PLAYSCRIPT 50

'the gymnasium' & other plays

THE TECHNICIANS
STAY WHERE YOU ARE
JACK THE GIANT-KILLER
NEITHER HERE NOR THERE

olwen wymark

CALDER AND BOYARS · LONDON

First published in Great Britain 1971
by Calder and Boyars Ltd
18 Brewer Street   London W1

© Olwen Wymark 1971

All performing rights in the plays are
strictly reserved and applications
for performances should be made to
Felix de Wolfe and Associates
61 Berkeley House
15 Hay Hill   London W1

No performance of the plays
may be given unless a licence has
been obtained prior to rehearsal

ALL RIGHTS RESERVED

ISBN 0 7145 0794 6 Cloth Edition
ISBN 0 7145 0795 4 Paper Edition

Any paperback edition of this book whether published
simultaneously with, or subsequent to, the hard bound
edition is sold subject to the condition that it shall not,
by way of trade, be lent, resold, hired out, or otherwise
disposed of, without the publishers' consent, in any form
of binding or cover other than that in which it is published

Printed by photo-lithography
and made in Great Britain at
The Pitman Press, Bath.

THE GYMNASIUM and other plays

This volume contains five further short plays by Olwen Wymark, author of Lunchtime Concert, Coda and The Inhabitants, which were published together as Playscript 3. They are beautifully observed pictures of human relationships, which are subtle, dramatic and intensely moving. Mrs. Wymark is a highly skilful, sensitive and original dramatist, whose works combine the rare delight of both reading well and playing well.

The Gymnasium is an extended metaphor concerning the deep insecurity of an older man married to a much younger wife: The Technicians is about evil and the kinds of alienation human beings allow to be practised on themselves: Stay Where You Are is about a young woman's gradual realisation, through benignly bizarre games, that her control of her life is illusory: Jack the Giant-Killer revolves around a young man in the act of freeing himself from the authority of the image of his parents: and Neither Here Nor There is concerned with the mystifications of the institutionalised elements of life today. Though they cover different subjects, they are united by the common themes of isolation and confusion they explore so variously and accurately. The Gymnasium was seen at the Traverse Theatre Club, Edinburgh, in 1967, The Technicians at the Phoenix Theatre, Leicester, in 1968, and Stay Where You Are and The Technicians in a double bill at The Traverse in 1969.

Olwen Wymark has also written several television plays. Her husband was the late Patrick Wymark, star of TV's The Power Game and countless stage and TV plays and films.

By the same author:

THREE PLAYS (Lunchtime Concert, The Inhabitants, Coda)

CONTENTS

THE GYMNASIUM	7
THE TECHNICIANS	21
STAY WHERE YOU ARE	67
JACK THE GIANT-KILLER	111
NEITHER HERE NOR THERE	123

This volume of plays is dedicated to Harold and to Patrick

THE GYMNASIUM

CHARACTERS

LEN

TONY

(The stage is empty. There is a rope stretched across the front of the stage between two poles to represent one side of a boxing ring. TONY, dressed in a towelling dressing gown strides in. He is about fifty - elegant, nervous, kind. He climbs over the ropes and begins earnestly and methodically to do some warming up exercises. LEN comes in from the other side. He is in a robe too with a towel round his neck. His hair is wet. He is about twenty five, well built and cheerful. Very friendly and resilient. He is a Cockney)

LEN. Hello Tone. How are you mate?

(TONY glances at him a bit distractedly but goes on doing his exercises and doesn't answer)

You're looking very good, Tone. Very very good. I'll have to watch myself today, eh?

(He too climbs into the ring. TONY leaves the rope and begins to prance up and down. Very serious and a bit breathless. LEN, facing him, starts bobbing up and down too)

(grinning) Shall we dance?

TONY. (standing still) Len...I'm awfully sorry. I don't mean to be rude, but do you mind not talking before we start? I'm afraid it really does interfere with my concentration.

LEN. Oh, sure mate. Sorry. Mum's the word, Tone.

TONY. You're sure you're not offended.

LEN. (very nice) A course not. This is your session.

TONY. You do understand?

LEN. Definitely Tone. Definitely I do. You about ready?

TONY. (hesitant) Yes I think so. (Then deep breath. Resolute) Yes.

(They take off their robes and LEN rubs his hair with the towel and then chucks it out of the ring. They are both in boxing shorts - TONY's rather quaint. LEN stands still in one corner smoothing down his hair. TONY goes to the other corner. LEN clears his throat and mutters a few phrases to himself. Then, gesturing to TONY apologetically, gets out some sheets of paper from his robe pocket. Checks through. Then closes his eyes. Mutters again. Then puts the sheets back. Straightens up. Clears his throat again)

LEN. Okay then. Here we go. Ding ding!

(They go into the centre and dance around each other ducking and feinting a bit)

How you ever got a driving licence I will never know.

TONY. I happen to be a very good driver.

LEN. Oh indeed? Is that so?

TONY. (punching and missing) Yes! As a matter of fact I used to do a bit of racing.

LEN. You...race! I didn't know they had racing cars thirty years ago.

TONY. It's not that long!

LEN. Oh I do beg your pardon. I thought you were fifty five now.

TONY. (desperate lunge) No I'm not. I'm fifty one.

LEN. (scathing) I've seen your passport.

TONY. (flailing punches) All right! All right! Fifty five!

LEN. Nearly fifty-six.

TONY. You knew how old I was when I married you.

LEN. At least you didn't lie about your age in those days.

(TONY starts to speak. Falters. Nearly stops moving)

LEN. (repeating as cue) At least you didn't lie about your age in those days.

(Again TONY tries to speak. Then suddenly he hides his face in his hands. After a bit he drops his hands and straightens up. LEN is watching, concerned)

TONY. (frank) It's no good. I'm just not getting it.

LEN. Sorry Cocker, my fault.

TONY. No no. Len, my dear chap. I assure you...

LEN. Straight up Tone, let's face it. I'm new to this sort of thing. You know. Bit out of my line. If I'm going wrong or if you'd like to try somebody else - you just say. Go on. You can tell me.

TONY. I would tell you, Len. I would. But it isn't you. No. It's me. As a matter of fact I think you've got a real natural gift, I really do. I hope you're not finding it an awful strain.

LEN. Oh no. I like it. I do, honest. Only I worry sometimes that I can't talk posh enough for the stuff you write for me. I bet she talks very posh. (Then almost to himself) She'd have to, some of the things she says. (Clicks his tongue, then cheerful, to TONY) I go through my bits (Gestures towards robe) at home the night before. It's a bit hard on the wife sometimes, though. She doesn't understand really, like...I'm going through some of it last week. I'm concentrating see. I don't even notice her. She's right in front of me and I say (Making a few punches as he speaks) 'What about women with wanted facial hair? She thought I was talking to her, see. She was very hurt...I mean, really cut up. You know.

TONY. (interested) Your wife has a moustache?

LEN. Yeah. Nice little one actually. I've always been very partial to it. But she bleaches it at night. Sensitive......

TONY. (indulgent. Smiling and shaking his head) Funny little thing.

LEN. Well...you know how they are.

TONY. (after a pause. Desperate) No!

(He goes to the rope and holds it with both hands, staring out at the audience. LEN watches him, perplexed and worried. He goes over to him and touches him gently. TONY jumps)

LEN. Easy, then, Tone. Easy. Let's go on, eh?

TONY. (effort at briskness) Yes. Yes. We'll go on.

LEN. Tell you what - let's just walk it for a bit. You know - like time before last. I'll start that long bit, shall I? Eh? That'll get you back into it. You'll see. Just take it slow.

TONY. (nods earnestly) Yes. Yes.

LEN. That's it. Here we go then.

(He starts to walk around the ring in a slow circle. TONY stands in the centre expectant and listening)

LEN. (not much expression yet. He is finding his way into the text) God knows no one could say you don't try. Eternal youth every day of the week for you. The hipster trousers, the flowered shirts, plastic ties... oh yes, oh yes the real 'gear'. How 'With it' can you get...at nearly sixty!

(It is at this point that TONY joins in the walking. He is still rather objective and nods to himself from time to time. They pace round and round getting a bit faster all the time)

Believe me, my friends can't wait to see what you're going to turn up in next. But don't think I haven't told them what you wear underneath. Laughs. Sorry Tone. (Then does laugh) Woollies, woollies, woollies all the year round! Nanny said, Mummy said, all your sisters always said 'Have you got your woollies on Anthony? You know how easily you get a chill on the tummy. Have you got your woollies on?

TONY. (precipitantly. Nearly missing his cue) Uh... I was a delicate child.

LEN. (own voice. Thumbs up to TONY) There you go, sailor. (Back to text) Child! You weren't a child at all! You were a short story by Emm Forster.

TONY. (rapidly but diffidently) Not Emm. E.M.

LEN. (over his shoulder) Eh?

TONY. E.M. Forster. Edward Morgan. He's a man.

LEN. Oh...sorry, cocker.

TONY. Doesn't matter a bit. Truly. Go on, Len. Go on.

LEN. (to self)...Uh...a short story by Eeeeee Emmm Forster...uh...uh...uh...

TONY. Would it be the bath next?

LEN. Oh yeah. Course.

>(He starts to move very fast now, zig zagging a bit. TONY begins to get emotionally very engaged. LEN's attitude throughout is of one doing a rather tricky job as well as he can. However, he appreciates a nice punchy text, so he says it energetically, always in Cockney and never effeminately)
>
>Do you think I don't know about the exercises you do on the bathroom floor? Do you really think I don't know that you splash your stomach with cold water before you get out of the bath. And why? Because your mother told you she always splashed her bust with cold water to firm it up. Doesn't work for Tony's tum tum, though, does it?

TONY. I don't do that...I don't! I admit I do think of it every time I get out of the bath but I don't actually do it.

LEN. (indifferent) What's the difference? Listen. When you stand up in the bath to get out do you look at yourself in the long mirror on the door?

TONY. (very defensive) Sometimes. Why shouldn't I?

LEN. I'll tell you what you do. You stand with your eyes closed and you reach around for your towel and you rub yourself all over very hard. And then you suck your stomach right in and you stand up as straight as a ramrod. You put on your - uh - enigmatic cowboy face and then you open your eyes and then you have a look. Not that you can really see without your glasses.

TONY. They're reading glasses. I've got very good vision.

LEN. Answer me one thing, Tony. Just answer me one question.

TONY. What? What question?

LEN. Who sees? Who's watching? Who gets a look at that

wonderful Hemingway hero? You – you're the only one that sees it and you know it's a lie.

TONY. (stopping dead) Yes! Yes! Go on!

LEN. (stopping and facing him across the ring) You haven't got any muscles! You're fat!

TONY. (eyes closed. Head up) Yes? Yes?

LEN. And flabby!

TONY. Yes?

LEN. You've got varicose veins and corns and hair in your nostrils!

TONY. Oh yes!

LEN. (own voice) Come on Tone, come on. Let me have it. It's time.

(TONY rushes blindly to him punching wildly. Some of the punches land)

That's it...that's it...Bony knees! Seven false teeth... that's the way...the bald patch...ouch!....Pow!... very good!

(Now TONY stands back panting. LEN is smiling encouragingly at him and still dancing round)

More?

TONY. More.

(LEN stops dancing and now prowls round TONY as he talks)

LEN. And what about your dancing, eh? Oh swinging Tony! Watching the kids dancing to pop on television. So solemn – you look like somebody decoding a secret message. All so you can ask someone's au pair girl to dance with you at a party.

TONY. You never dance with me.

LEN. Me? (Laughs) No thank you. Sweating and puffing and snapping your fingers.

TONY. Well why do you always egg me on to dance at parties?

LEN. Because it makes me laugh. You're so funny!

TONY. You think I'm old fashioned is that it?

LEN. That's it.

TONY. Old fashioned and ridiculous.

LEN. Ridiculous.

TONY. You laugh at me. You watch me and - and talk about me - and laugh with other people.

LEN. Of course. Look at Tony...isn't he heaven? Oh, look, look! He's doing his Antonio bit. (LEN does burlesque flamenco dancing) Yes, he's divine isn't he? Such a darling old pet. Marvellous for his age. Oh didn't you? Well, he's fifty-five - yes, isn't it amazing? Fifty-five! (Shouts this)

TONY. You tell people!

LEN. (matter of fact) Always.

(There is a short pause. They stand still facing each other. Then LEN relaxes, rubs his hair with the flat of his hand. TONY hasn't moved. He stands straight, his face expressionless)

Well, I guess that's it, then. Curtain down, eh?

(TONY doesn't move or respond)

It's the end of what you gave me, Tone. It seemed to me it finished a bit sudden, but that was all there was......

(He turns away from TONY and leans over the rope to reach for his towel)

But it went okay I thought, didn't you? You were doing some beautiful work in there, Tone. Terrific. I thought to myself, 'Ayup, it won't be that long before he'll be marking me for fair'. I did, honest...

(He still has his back to TONY and is starting to put on his robe when TONY strides swiftly over to him, seizes him and throws him onto the floor, in the centre of the ring)

Hey...Tone! Wotcha doing?

TONY. (standing over him and paying no attention to his expostulations) You don't love me. You never loved me. You despise me!

LEN. Wait a minute...I don't know this bit...

TONY. (overriding) It's no good, I tell you. It doesn't fool me any more. It's just a charade. You pretend to love me, you pretend to admire me. You laugh at all my jokes, you quote me to other people, but it's all mocking. I can see that now. You do it for fun!

(He kneels down by LEN who is a bit dazed and just stares at him)

Yes I believed you. I wanted to believe you. I needed to. It was like a miracle. Thirty years younger and yet you loved me. I used to look at your smooth little face, your beautiful solid little body and I believed that you were mine. Go ahead...laugh! I believed you had been given to me by God to make me able to believe in myself. Go on...laugh at me! Laugh at me!

LEN. (very confused) I wouldn't laugh at you, Tone. You

know that.

(TONY turns away from him. He is kneeling and swaying. He looks rather absurd, but his anguish is very strong and entirely felt)

TONY. Oh how could you, how could you? I can't forget anything - even if they were lies. Those secret little kisses on my neck when no one was looking. Holding onto my coat when we crossed a street, sitting on the floor and watching me with those big eyes when I talked...I could tell by your face that I was saying wonderful things. And now I know (Starts to weep) you were biting back the laughter all the time. Old ugly foolish Tony. Everyone will understand when you leave him. Why did you marry him in the first place? Why? Why? (He buries his face in his hands and sobs)

(LENNY raises himself and looks at TONY. Then he crawls over to him and crouches beside him, his face full of sympathy and sadness)

LEN. (very gentle. Putting his arms round TONY) All right, Tone. It's all right mate. Come on. Come on. It's all right. Don't cry.

(TONY looks up at him. LEN takes TONY's face in his hands and pats his cheeks, smooths back his hair and wipes away some tears with his fingers)

Listen Tone, you mustn't get so upset. I have to tell you this 'cause it's on my mind every time. Every time we have a session. You're too good for her. She's a bitch. I tell you Tone, she's a right bitch. You're a very respectable man - very intelligent and very good-looking, I mean that. People look up to you. Believe me, Tone, I've always been very proud to work with you. You got to have faith in yourself, mate, no matter what happens to you. All right, your wife's leaving you. Good riddance, that's what I say.

TONY. (flat. Tired) She isn't leaving me.

LEN. What? After all the horrible things she said to you...

TONY. She didn't say them.

LEN. How do you mean, Tone? I don't get you.

TONY. She doesn't say them. She never never says anything unkind or cruel to me. But you see, Len, I know (Looking earnestly into LEN's face) I <u>know</u> she's thinking them. (He gets up and turns away from LEN) If only she'd say them. Oh God, if only she'd say them!

(Blackout)

CURTAIN

THE TECHNICIANS

THE TECHNICIANS was first presented by The Voyage Theatre Company at The Phoenix Theatre, Leicester, on February 4th, 1969, with the following cast:

STARR	Harold Lang
JORDAN	David Kelsey
MRS. RUST	Helen Dorward
MR. RUST	Nicholas Amer
ROLAND BATE	Greville Hallam

The play was directed by Tony Tanner and Harold Lang.

(Station waiting room. There are two men. One, JORDAN, is half lying on a bench. The other, STARR, is standing still, his back to the audience. JORDAN is older than STARR. STARR howls like a wolf and then is still. JORDAN doesn't move. His eyes are closed)

JORDAN. (mild) Go on.

STARR. The boredom! The dead air! The grit!

JORDAN. (still eyes closed) Good.

STARR. I can't sleep!

JORDAN. (sits up and looks at him. Still mild. Interested) Why?

STARR. I'm too tired. (Pause. Violently) I hate the coffee!

JORDAN. Because... ?

STARR. Because it's like mud puddles heated up and disinfected.

JORDAN. (smiles slightly) Not bad. And?

STARR. The noise of trains, loud speakers, feet, porters' carts, bells, whistles, people! I hate them all!

JORDAN. (nods) You hate them all.

STARR. (turns swiftly then runs round to face JORDAN)

Yes!

JORDAN. (returns his gaze attentively) Better?

(There is a pause. JORDAN continues to gaze kindly at STARR. STARR brought up short and frozen in a position with an element of threat in it stares somewhat wildly back at him. Then he drops his eyes, shrugs, smiles, brushes himself down with his hands and executes a little tap dance)

STARR. Much better thanks.

JORDAN. (gets up and strolls past STARR patting his shoulder as he passes him) There would appear to be an element of strain.

STARR. (following him) No, no.

JORDAN. The job, after all, is not an easy one...God knows. (He laughs very heartily and after a slight pause STARR joins in) And you are, of course, relatively inexperienced.

STARR. (a little anxious) Yes, that's true, but I assure you Jordan, I know I can do it.

JORDAN. (reassuring) Of course you can. That's why you were selected. I think it's nothing to worry about. Don't let your mind dwell on it. (Gently) Just relax. We all go through these phases of...uncertainty. It's almost inevitable in an early assignment - Ah! Someone's coming!

(Swiftly they both sit down and at once feign sleep)

WOMAN'S VOICE OFF. In here do you mean?

MAN OFF. Obviously.

WOMAN. (opening door and coming in) Obvious to some.

(THE MAN follows her in. She is middle-aged in a fur

coat and a not quite fashionable hat. He is small and something of a dandy. They are MR. and MRS. RUST)

MR. RUST. There. Now that's a very good example of what I was mentioning. You say, 'Obvious to some'. What does that mean? It doesn't mean anything. It's just showing off - enigmatically showing off.

MRS. RUST. Be quiet! There are people over there.

MR. RUST. They're asleep.

MRS. RUST. I don't see that that makes any difference. I'm not washing my dirty linen - or rather your dirty linen - in front of other people, awake or asleep.

MR. RUST. (taking up a rather elaborately negligent pose by the mantelpiece) Quite an interesting point, that. Actually, we are never interested in other people's reactions to us. That is to say, it is always of great importance to give a good impression but it is really more to impress ourselves and not the others. I would rather, for example, die than have the milkman see me without my hair piece - although I have no interest in the milkman at all nor he in me. If he came and found me hanging from the ceiling in the front hall one morning, he would be interested but not sorry.

MRS. RUST. The same would apply to you if it were he that was hanging.

MR. RUST. Not quite. I would not even be interested; I would be irritated. (Pause) Why then do I rush into my toupee if I know I am going to encounter him?

MRS. RUST. (smilingly unkind) Why indeed? You look better without it anyway.

MR. RUST. (taking a step forward and speaking anxiously) You really do think that?

MRS. RUST. I really do.

(MR. RUST turns, takes off his hat and regards himself
very carefully in the dim mirror over the mantelpiece)

MR. RUST. I wish I knew if I should take it to heart when
you say that.

MRS. RUST. (scornful) Heart...hah! (Then looks round at
JORDAN and STARR and repeats in a whisper) Hah!
Will you kindly remember that we are not alone.

MR. RUST. The point is, we are. Just as I am with the
milkman - if you follow me.

MRS. RUST. I don't. (Moves away from him. Walks about)
Must we continue to speak of the milkman? I am here.
Isn't that, for the moment, enough?

MR. RUST. (quickly) We are both here. (Pause) Simply
going away for a few days.

MRS. RUST. (glancing at him) Simply.

MR. RUST. To stay with the Stringers. It must be five
years since we saw them.

MRS. RUST. Or ten. Or possibly fifteen.

(Suddenly she walks swiftly to the door of the waiting
room. MR. RUST half rises from his chair. Watches
her. She stops at the door. Turns and walks back
again. Relieved he sits again. Then once more she
wheels about and makes for the door. Again he rises.
Watches. She stops. Waits. Then walks slowly back
into the room. She sits)

MR. RUST. (crossing his legs. Smiling and pedantic) The
question as I say of the impression we might make
on other people has nothing of altruism in it. You and
I, for example, would refrain from any - mm - fierce
discussion in front of other people. Why? To avoid
seeing on their faces any expression of disapproval
which might undermine our own self esteem. 'When
in disgrace with fortune and men's _eyes_' d'you see.

>What they are <u>thinking</u> is of no interest whatever to us. We have no protective impulses concerning their ideals about the dignity or grace of mankind. Certainly we would be in no way engaged in sparing their sensibilities -

MRS. RUST. You would not. No.

MR. RUST. (edgy) Nor would you. Your interest in other people is so marginal it is practically off the page.

MRS. RUST. I suppose you regard that as an epigram.

MR. RUST. Your interest in other people's interest in you, however, is radiantly central.

MRS. RUST. Whereas you -

MR. RUST. (gets up hastily) No no, please. Don't misunderstand me. I do not speak punitively - not at all. Simply an observation and, as you pointed out so accurately -

MRS. RUST. And humanely.

MR. RUST. (disconcerted) Pardon?

MRS. RUST. As I pointed out so accurately <u>and</u> humanely.

MR. RUST. (rather depressed) Oh dear.

>(There is a silence. Then MR. RUST turns and looks at her)

>What about the dog, for example? What happened to the dog?

MRS. RUST. (bland) He set himself on fire as a protest against the Americans.

MR. RUST. (scathing smile) Set himself...?

MRS. RUST. I always knew exactly what he was thinking.

It was what he would have wanted. We were very close.

MR. RUST. (taken aback) You hated the dog!

MRS. RUST. (calm) Yes. But we were very close.

(Again a pause)

MR. RUST. I wonder if you have ever considered why you picked up all those things on the beach in Corsica. Sticks and stones. No shells. Weapons I would say.

MRS. RUST. (tense) Not weapons. No.

MR. RUST. Oh I think yes - though indeed perhaps only on an unconscious level. Such large stones some of them, after all.

MRS. RUST. (gets up. She is agitated and speaks now with real personal sincerity) You couldn't possibly understand. To me stones are full of mystery - secrets...

MR. RUST. Secrets from whom pray?

MRS. RUST. No <u>from</u> anyone. When you hold a stone in your hand there's something positive and truthful about it. It feels heavy and warm and safe. And the driftwood...It's smooth and strange and yet at the same time...familiar. (She holds up one of her hands. The other circling its wrist and looks at it trying to find the right words) It's like...it's like...

(STARR gets up and breaks in on her speech. He holds his hands just as she is doing)

STARR. Like a bone.

JORDAN. (gets up and moves towards him) Quite. Bone. Quite. Weapon.

STARR. Not at all. Not a weapon. No. A bone is a reason and a meaning.

JORDAN. And there you go enigmatically showing off again. You judge me by yourself. When I am trying seriously to talk about something, you think it is as trivial as you and the milkman and your toupee.

STARR. And you think the milkman and I and my toupee are trivial.

JORDAN. Yes I do.

STARR. Once more ill met by moonlight, proud Titania. I find the whole question of the milkman vis a vis my toupee large and interesting and rather sad.

MRS. RUST. (whispering to MR. RUST) Tell them to stop!

MR. RUST. You tell them.

MRS. RUST. It's you who should. I'm a woman.

JORDAN. (to STARR) A woman! Easy to say.

STARR. (to JORDAN) Harder to say than man; harder to be than man.

JORDAN. I'm not at all sure you are a woman.

STARR. (pleasantly) Well certainly you have done little practical research on the question for the past five years.

JORDAN. Don't be coarse.

STARR. You think all facts are coarse. You think a bald head is coarse.

JORDAN. Not coarse - triste. It's a French word; it means sad.

STARR. I am aware of that, as it happens.

JORDAN. You understand definitions - not meanings.

(STARR puts up his hand to prevent JORDAN speaking)

STARR. Wait. Wait.

> (He goes to the centre of the stage and slowly and well executes an arabesque. JORDAN watches. MR. and MRS. RUST move forward a little to see. Then STARR breaks the pose and turns smiling to look at them all)

JORDAN. Bravo! Bravo! Thanks very much. I say, I really can't tell you...

STARR. (pleased but modest) No no, please. It was nothing.

> (Now JORDAN and STARR turn to face MR. and MRS. RUST)

JORDAN. (friendly) Well, what did you think?

MR. RUST. Mmmmm...think?

MRS. RUST. Well if you want to know what I think -

MR. RUST. No I don't think we do.

JORDAN. Excuse me, but we do - definitely we do. (Polite gesture to MRS. RUST)

MRS. RUST. (rather grand) I think you're both very impertinent. Both of you - very very impertinent.

STARR. (nods affably) Yes I see.

JORDAN. Of course. It's a very good point. Awfully good. (Smiles again) My name is Jordan. My colleague - Starr. (He and STARR bow politely)

> (MR. and MRS. RUST look confused. Then MR. RUST collects himself and takes off his hat)

MR. RUST. My name is Rust. And this is my wife, Mrs.

Rust.

(Again JORDAN and STARR bow. There is another pause in which JORDAN and STARR gaze expectantly at the RUSTS who look rather blankly and nervously back at them)

JORDAN. (diffident and courteous) Well it really is your turn isn't it? I don't like to rush you, but one of our trains may be coming in at any moment. Where are you going, if I may ask?

MR. RUST. Mmm...Crewe...actually...

JORDAN. Ah. We are going to St. Pancras.

MRS. RUST. But this is St. Pancras.

JORDAN. Yes, we arrived last night.

STARR. But it will take a good deal longer to get here this time.

JORDAN. Oh yes. Two or three days I should say - at a rough guess.

MR. RUST. You...mmm...work for the railway?

JORDAN. (smilingly explanatory) Well not so much 'for' as 'during'.

(STARR now begins to clap his hands raised up and directed towards the RUSTS. Friendly and encouraging)

MRS. RUST. Why is he doing that?

JORDAN. Well he wants you to begin.

MRS. RUST. Begin what?

JORDAN. Oh anything...a song, a little dancing, an exchange of words, a shaggy dog story; really anything you feel up to.

MR. RUST. Now look here...I mean to say...This is a station waiting room you know, not a circus. We don't have to -

(MRS. RUST interrupting and singing very sweetly)

MRS. RUST. Follow follow follow follow follow follow follow me.

MR. RUST. (joining in rather unwilling and embarrassed. Again just tips his hat) Follow follow follow follow follow follow follow me.

MRS. RUST.
Whither shall I follow follow thee?
Whither shall I follow follow thee?

MR. RUST.
Whither shall I follow follow thee?
Whither shall I follow follow thee?

MRS. RUST.
To the greenwood, to the greenwood, to the greenwood greenwood tree.

MR. RUST.
To the greenwood, to the greenwood, to the greenwood greenwood tree.

(This is a round so MR. RUST finishes with the last line solo. JORDAN and STARR applaud enthusiastically. MR. and MRS. RUST look both pleased and abashed. Suddenly the door opens and a YOUNG MAN comes in very fast. He is drunk but it shows in his intensity and extravagance rather than in imprecision of movement or articulation)

MRS. RUST. (shocked and loud) What are _you_ doing here?

(There is a brief pause and everyone turns to look at him)

MAN. Following you. What else would I be doing?

MRS. RUST. How dare you! How dare you follow me!

(The young man, ROLAND CAT, crosses swiftly to her and takes her roughly by the shoulders)

ROLAND. I warned you.

MRS. RUST. (flat and low) Go away.

ROLAND. (low voice but vicious intensity) You were wrong, weren't you? I told you you couldn't walk out on me. A second honeymoon with your lawful spouse was that it? A fresh start with me tidied out of the way? Sorry to spoil your plans.

MRS. RUST. (tired) Leave me.

ROLAND. (close into her. Hard) <u>When I want to.</u> Not before.

(At this point MR. RUST springs forward. Speaks to JORDAN and STARR)

MR. RUST. A nephew. My wife's nephew, Roland Cat.

(JORDAN and STARR have been watching with warm interest. They nod. ROLAND wheels round to look at them. Throws back his head and laughs)

ROLAND. That's right. I just came to say goodbye. Roly's going to miss his Auntie.

(MR. RUST moves over to MRS. RUST)

MR. RUST. (low) I must apologise. An impulse - an undisciplined impulse.

ROLAND. (confidentially to JORDAN and STARR. Speaks through laughter) I don't know how well you know my

Aunt, but we're all frightfully worried about her - the whole family. It's rotten for my...uncle. You see she's not true to him. She has love affairs all the time. I <u>think</u> he knows about it...

JORDAN. (steps forward, raises clenched fist and speaks very sonorously to STARR) Know? Know? Thinkest thou, base foolish woman, that I am blind to thy deceit?

STARR. (adopting the same style) How deceit? I understand thee not. Thy meaning is dark to me.

(ROLAND has flopped onto the bench and watches this, bemused. The RUSTS have turned to listen too)

JORDAN. It is thou whose meaning is dark - dark in thy soul. Woman - thou hast betrayed me.

STARR. Never!

JORDAN. Betrayed me. False to me I say, and not once but many times.

MRS. RUST. (agitated) And what's all that about you cheeky devils. We're not interested in all this silliness and rubbish. I'll thank you-

MR. RUST. (interrupting her. Very discomfited) No need to pay attention to them, no need at all. They're obviously a little... (Touches his forehead)

MRS. RUST. You're right. Of course they are. Come along, we'll -

(They start for the door but STARR's speech arrests them)

STARR. False? False to thee? Go riddle with the Gods. Thou <u>art</u> falsehood. Thou art a bank of shifting sand, the smouldering light before the thunderstorm glowing with seeming truth but followed by rattling chaos. To betray thee is but to honour clarity.

JORDAN. O shield thyself. Stoop, stoop and cover thy head with embracing arms. If mine own wrath doth not strike thee, surely the Gods themselves will crush thee for thine insolence.

STARR. None but thou couldst confound insolence with despair.

JORDAN. Speakest thou - <u>worm</u> - of despair? It is I, not thou who am wronged. <u>I,</u> the dupe of thy transgression.

STARR. Blind thou art indeed to designate it so - transgression.

JORDAN. Thou dare deny thy trespass?

STARR. No trespass. Like to the vixen started from her lair, alone I fled. Thou, my protector and my safety, transformed into the baying pack hounding me into the anarchic forest. It was I had become the victim. Thy terror and thy doubt menaced me.

JORDAN. Menaced thee? I, thy lord?

STARR. Yes thou. When first thou camest to me, thou saidst I was a stripling birch tree, my thin gold sap rising with hope toward the sun. Thou saw'st that either side me two gnarled and cankered parent trees robbed me of my light, my hope of growth. Thou, my love, - aye, my lord to be - camest to save me, vowed to show me mine own beauty and my truth.

JORDAN. And kept that vow. Dost dare to say I hindered thee?

STARR. Yes, yes! Thy terror I say; I say thy terror hindered me. How might I trust any new shoot of my own when the whole shaft of thy being was eaten soft and pulpy with suspicion.

JORDAN. I did not suspect thee then. Not then.

STARR. Thyself, it was thyself that thou suspected. Thou

wast for me the doorkeeper to disorder. Thou gazed fearfully on life itself and doubted it. And in this manner didst thou unlock that door for me which opened onto a desert. Here in the half dark on this arid plain littered with broken buildings and mutilated creatures I have wandered searching for certainty. No shelter here - no safety. I am alone. The hard earth mutters under my feet. My Odyssey is endless and full of threatening singing shapes. Yes! I must play Ulysses' part. (Then bitterly and straight to JORDAN's face) While my <u>Penelope</u> sits safe the other side the door picking and unpicking.

JORDAN. (after a brief pause steps forward and speaks in a low kind voice to STARR) We demonstrate - do <u>not</u> participate. (And he smilingly shakes STARR lightly by the shoulders)

MRS. RUST. Don't touch me!

ROLAND. (puzzled. Frightened) Who's touching <u>you</u>?

MR. RUST. (stepping forward. Embarrassed. Speaks to JORDAN and STARR) I'm afraid my wife is implacably romantic. She visits the cinema a great deal...gets very involved, you know...quite...mmm...committed.

JORDAN. Of course. Perfectly natural.

STARR. And very healthy too.

MR. RUST. Healthy?

JORDAN. Certainly. The aim here is to intensify, inflate, you might say, thereby effecting some sort of disseverance - a bird's eye view. However, it's entirely natural and (Nod to STARR) healthy that when the centre of feeling is disturbed, it can be difficult for a subject to remain altogether disengaged or -

STARR. Detached.

JORDAN. Exactly. But after regular practice it becomes

possible to achieve the one remove. Although the work is arduous, we have always found it useful.

STARR. Ameliorative.

JORDAN. The intention, you see, is simply to lift an experience or a set of feelings from the practical or market-place reality onto a level of - well you could call it melodrama.

STARR. Super-charged. Transcendental.

JORDAN. Or what might be more simply called Grand Guignol.

STARR. It's an awfully effective way of alleviating discomfort.

JORDAN. (genial) And fun too, after all. Eloquence and passion - very heady stuff.

MR. RUST. You mean make a joke of it. A mockery.

JORDAN. Oh no. A pleasantry.

MR. RUST. But belittling surely.

JORDAN. That does come into it of course.

STARR. Willy nilly.

(ROLAND has become more apprehensive and confused as they have been speaking. He shrinks into the corner of the bench, crouched over, hugging himself with his arms as he watches. Suddenly he jumps up and bends over. He finds the shape of a giant spider and then with great rapidity he scuttles over to MRS. RUST, around her, then round the whole stage this way and that. He comes back to the bench, swiftly uncoils up to a sitting position and crosses his legs. They are all standing stock still staring at him. He looks round at them, nervy and irritated. It is obvious that he is totally unaware of this piece of unconscious 'acting out')

ROLAND. Well, what are you all looking at me for?

STARR. (gently. Interested) Why did you do that?

ROLAND. Do what?

STARR. All that crouching and rushing...this.

(He gets down and imitates ROLAND's movements)

ROLAND. Are you out of your mind?

JORDAN. (going over to him) Quite right - he does it badly. Believe me I'm quite sincere when I say I can't imagine anyone doing it anything like as well as you. Absolutely definitive. It's impertinent of me I know, but could you tell us a bit about the source for the idea?

ROLAND. What idea? I don't know what the hell you're talking about.

STARR. Spider, I should say.(Then to MR. RUST) Wouldn't you?

MR. RUST. (speaking rather suddenly) Or a road.

ROLAND. (jumping up) Who are you calling a toad you little...

STARR. Oh much too light and swift for a toad. Look. He was suggesting a sort of circular movement. (Bends down and does it again)

JORDAN. How can you possibly explain the terrific speed in that case? Your 'circular movement' just hampers. No no, it was based on diagonals. (He too gets down and joins STARR in showing)

ROLAND. Stop! Stop it! What are you doing?

MR. RUST. (glances at ROLAND and smiles so slightly it hardly shows. Then rubs his hands together briskly) Well I may not know much about it but the whole thing

reminded me sharply of the American Horned Toad.
(He too gets down and holds a crouched pose) Imagine
a tiny dinosaur with angry popping eyes. (He begins to
scuttle about)

(Now all three of them are rushing and darting around
the stage. ROLAND watches with astonishment, then
terror. MRS. RUST watches ROLAND anxiously)

ROLAND. (crying out to her) What do they mean? What are
they doing? I didn't do anything like that. I didn't, did
I?

MRS. RUST. (moving to him arms outstretched) Of course
not. Of course you didn't.

(ROLAND runs to her, kneels and puts his arms around
her hiding his face in her. The others watch. MR.
RUST, upset and confused, moves to the fireplace and
occupies himself with minute alterations to his toupee,
his tie)

ROLAND. It's dark, it's dark. The room is full of horrible
things moving around.

MRS. RUST. No, no, there is nothing there. It's only your
imagination.

ROLAND. I can hear noises.

MRS. RUST. It's only the floor creaking and the wind in
the trees outside.

ROLAND. Did you hear what they said? I didn't do <u>any</u>-
thing. They were lying.

MRS. RUST. Of course they were, the sillies.

ROLAND. Why are people always telling lies about me?
They talk about me behind my back, I know that.
They say vicious things about me. I know they all hate
me.

MRS. RUST. (turns his face up to her. Warm and comforting. During all this section she is more mother/nanny than lover) They don't hate you, they're afraid of you. You're brave and handsome. You have wit. You're elegant and wise. There is no one in the world like you.

ROLAND. No one?

MRS. RUST. No one at all. You are the only one.

(ROLAND looks up at her and slowly moves his hands up to cover her breasts)

ROLAND. I love you.

(JORDAN and STARR, after a little pause, move forward. They laugh with warm and friendly appreciation)

STARR. (pleased. Sincere) Delightful.

JORDAN. Really charming. It would make a wonderful musical. I wonder if you'd do it again. So nice...

(MRS. RUST and ROLAND, heedless, continue to look at each other)

Well. I think this is a point for examination. (To STARR) Wouldn't you say?

STARR. Why not?

(They both clap their hands. MRS. RUST and ROLAND start. Look at them)

JORDAN. Now, if the jury would just...

(He goes over to ROLAND and MRS. RUST and leads them to one of the benches at the side. He seats them and then motions MR. RUST to join them. STARR moves to stand behind the centre chair, his hands resting on the back as if it were a witness box)

JORDAN. (to the others) Thanks so much. That's perfect. Please feel quite free to take notes.

(Then he begins to walk about, eyeing STARR, his thumbs in his waistcoat pocket)

There were definite avowals, you say, of love.

STARR. On many occasions.

JORDAN. Perhaps you could give me an approximate number.

STARR. I could not. They were countless.

JORDAN. Again we find ourselves without facts. I submit that this relationship exists only on a fantasy wish level in your mind.

STARR. That's not true.

JORDAN. You are forty-five years of age?

STARR. That is correct.

JORDAN. And the plaintiff is twenty two years old. Is that true?

STARR. I believe that is so.

JORDAN. Half your own age - not half. And you say this - young person - made repeated declarations of love to you?

STARR. I do.

JORDAN. I put it to you, ladies and gentlemen of the jury, could such an association possibly have existed? One so incongruous... so grotesque? I suggest rather that the young man in question came to this woman in all innocence - seeking friendship. A person so much older than himself might advise and instruct, be an influence for good. But instead... what? An ageing woman, hungry and frustrated, fastens on him, her own demands like insatiable leeches drain away his manhood and his integrity. Lust is the word here, ladies and gentlemen; lust, not love.

(MRS. RUST stands up making some inarticulate sound)

(Smiling and putting a hand out towards her) A moment... please.

(He goes upstage, stands with his back to the audience for a moment and then turns round and comes back to STARR)

(Now as lawyer for the defence) Forgive me if this is painful for you, but my honourable colleague has implied a rapacious seduction on your part. Could you, in your own words, tell the court your view of the relationship between yourself and the plaintiff.

STARR. (lofty. A bit absurd) We were lovers.

JORDAN. And how did this begin?

STARR. (he begins this speech in a rather pedantic way but as he goes on he becomes involved and serious) With seduction, yes that is true, but it was he who seduced me. I was at the time we met very melancholy and oppressed. He was...is...deeply engrossed in sensuality, a thing that has always unnerved me. His hot insistence conquered my fear. I submitted. And in this submission - perhaps the first real submission of my life... (His face becomes puzzled and he speaks haltingly) I found...refreshment, light and peace.

(Then very softly, involuntarily and under her breath MRS. RUST sings)

MRS. RUST. Follow follow follow follow follow follow follow me.

(There is a silence. STARR looks at MRS. RUST. JORDAN looks shrewdly at STARR)

JORDAN. (coming very close to STARR and speaking softly) Be careful.

STARR. What do you mean?

JORDAN. (smiles) The strain we spoke of previously, you remember? Don't forget...detachment.

STARR. (edgy) I don't know what you mean. I'm perfectly detached. You're bullying me.

JORDAN. Yes.

(There is a pause while they look at each other. Then JORDAN resumes the barrister pose)

(Ironic. Smiling) Refreshment? Light? Peace?

STARR. (shakes his head to collect himself. Then speaks in a sarcastic and unpleasant voice) And trouble.

JORDAN. Enlarge.

STARR. I said trouble. Inconvenience, tedium, alarm. Rage, despair, drunkenness, scenes, broken crockery, black eyes, pettiness.

JORDAN. Perhaps a concrete example...

STARR. If I might be permitted to call a witness.

JORDAN. By all means.

(STARR gets up and goes to MRS. RUST and holds out his hand)

MRS. RUST. Me?

JORDAN. If you wouldn't mind.

ROLAND. Well she would mind. (Then urgently to MRS. RUST) You don't have to do anything. I know all about these people. I've read about them. Psychedelic

Private Eyes. They have no authority.

STARR. (shrugs and walks back to his chair. His tone is a little bored) On one occasion I was forced to call the police. Windows were being broken, unbelievable obscenities shouted, no, screamed, in the street. 'Dangerous lunatic' they said. They were right.

MRS. RUST. (half rising) Wrong! Wrong!

ROLAND. (vociferously to STARR) You see - you see! Why don't you keep your mouth shut you crummy little prick.

(STARR goes over to him smiling with broad pleasure. He and JORDAN exchange an enthusiastic nod and JORDAN rubs his hands together in a brisk and jolly manner. He walks over to ROLAND)

JORDAN. Well, this is nice. Do go on.

(STARR claps his hands encouragingly)

ROLAND. (looks from one to the other with nervous dislike and sits down) I'm not saying another word. You can't fool me.

JORDAN. (very affable) Perhaps later.

STARR. Plenty of time.

JORDAN. (to STARR) I think if we were just to pick up where we -

STARR. The wisest course. (Walks back to chair talking as he goes) Certainly there is no doubt that he was in need of psychiatric attention. The drinking problem aside, there was the paranoia, the frequent delusions of grandeur, the aggressive outbursts against authority of any kind...Oh indeed yes, a deeply unstable personality -

MRS. RUST. That's not fair. It isn't fair to say it that

way. (Gets up and walks hurriedly over to the bench and stands opposite STARR) You're leaving too much out.

STARR. Quite right. There are far worse things I should have mentioned. Of course there is no point now in omitting any detail, no matter how vile.

MRS. RUST. That's not what I mean. You're leaving out... what you <u>omit</u> is the real person.

STARR. (didactic) The reality of a person is what he does and what he says.

MRS. RUST. (going round the chair towards him) Not to someone who loves him.

(The moment she steps behind the chair, STARR moves away and he and JORDAN turn up to face her. Now she is in 'the witness box')

JORDAN. Would it then be fair to assume, Madam, that in your view 'the eyes of love are blind'?

(Now MRS. RUST realises where she is. She is embarrassed but shows that she feels the questions must be answered)

MRS. RUST. (low but positive) No. No.

STARR. Blind at any rate to the faults of the - uh - Loved One?

MRS. RUST. (bit impatient) The question of faults doesn't come into it.

JORDAN. The person in question is you would say a man composed entirely of virtues?

MRS. RUST. There aren't any faults <u>or</u> any virtues. There is only the person himself. You d<u>on</u>'t assess...you see.

STARR. See everything except the black eyes and broken

crockery?

MRS. RUST. You see what is. Not what you think about what is, or what the world thinks, or what might have been or what ought to be. You simply see.

JORDAN. (shakes his head, smiles, speaks emphatically, separating the words) Not - possible - no.

MRS. RUST. Yes. (Continues with some effort) To love is to bear witness to the possibility of another person. To outside eyes that other person may seem silly, selfish, tedious, greedy, dangerous or dull. His words and his actions may often antagonise or irritate. Other people may pity him, deplore him, even despise him.

JORDAN. (smoothly) With reason.

STARR. (glancing benignly at ROLAND) With good reason.

MRS. RUST. (continues as though there had been no interruption) And five minutes after he has left their field of vision, they are indifferent to him; they have forgotten him. The one who loves him never forgets him. Everything seen, felt or heard reminds - partakes - of the beloved.

JORDAN. No judgement then?

MRS. RUST. Never any judgement.

STARR. Excuses are always found?

MRS. RUST. Not excuses - causes. There is no word that can be spoken, no action performed by the beloved that cannot attentively be traced to some place of pain or uncertainty.

STARR. Or lust. (Lingers nastily on the word)

MRS. RUST. (simply. Making the word beautiful) Or lust. The true lover has made entrance to the labyrinth of another. Here is the image and likeness of God.

(JORDAN and STARR laugh with great pleasure)

(Again quite heedless of them) Only the lover knows of the beloved that he is, that he is he, that he is only he and that only he is he.

STARR. Just a sec. Have I got that right? (Gabbles) That he is only? Only he is only that? He only is only is?

MRS. RUST. (not to him but just repeating with peaceful clarity) That he is. That he is he. That he is only he and that only he is he.

STARR. Oh gracious, I'll never remember all that.

MRS. RUST. Within this place of recognition and celebration, there are no questions that cannot be answered. There are no questions to be asked.

JORDAN. The...lover... (Politely questioning look to make sure he has the word right) sees all, hears all, knows all?

MRS. RUST. (mild) No. Perceives the possibility of all.

STARR. (moves away and speaks now in strong Cockney. Pompously sagacious) Well I may not have had much of what you call education and I'm not much on all these fancy terms, but I've seen a lot of people come and go. I'd say I'd a fair amount of experience. One thing I will say about myself I am a good judge of character. It doesn't take me five minutes before I can tell you pretty well what kind of a bloke a man is.

JORDAN. (also Cockney) Bloke? You gone blind? This (indicating MRS. RUST) ain't a bloke. It's a she.

STARR. (finger on nose. Very knowing) Ah, you can't always tell you know. I had a uncle used to look very much like that.

(They look at MRS. RUST in silence for a moment)

JORDAN. Yeah, but this one's got a skirt on and stockings and that.

STARR. That don't prove nothing. My uncle used to dress like that...only better. Very snappy dresser, my uncle. Ankle strap shoes I remember, and lots of rhinestone bracelets...that sort of stuff...you know - class.

JORDAN. Well you're right. This one hasn't got much what you might call taste.

STARR. Taste! This one wouldn't know the meaning of the word.

JORDAN. Will you look at that bleeding hat! (He snatches it off MRS. RUST and throws it to STARR who puts it on)

STARR. (exaggerated aristocratic voice) Ladies! We must face facts. In this village alone, leaving aside for the moment the rest of the country, at least 75,000 earthworms a month are mercilessly maimed or slaughtered. In the name of humanity we must act. May I have a motion for a petition to be sent to her gracious majesty...

JORDAN. (laughing and grabbing the hat from him. Puts it on) No, you got it all wrong. (As a fairly drunken lady) Oh well, I'll have a teeney, weeney gin if I may. I don't really drink you know, but as it's a party... Gracious, aren't you a charming boy!

STARR. (going over close to JORDAN) You like me lady? Five quid and I'll come back to your place, eh? Would you like that?

JORDAN. (running a hand down STARR's back and thigh) My goodness I don't know what you mean...you little rascal. (Rubs up against STARR) Besides I haven't got five pounds.

STARR. Well for two pounds ten I could - (Whispers into

JORDAN's ear)

(JORDAN shouts with laughter. He takes off the hat and chucks it into a corner and he and STARR laugh together. MRS. RUST has remained impassive through all this. ROLAND and MR. RUST seem mesmerised watching all this but now MR. RUST scuttles after the hat, picks it up, dusts it off etc.
Now JORDAN and STARR start moving round MRS. RUST. They half crouch as they move and take turns making remarks but although the tone is lewd and obscene we can't hear the words. They punctuate the phrases with a rising nasty laughter. They nearly touch her but don't quite. JORDAN says something...a question)

(Clearly. Still Cockney) Well let's have a look, shall we?

JORDAN. Bring in the cameras, men. We're going to have a little closeup on a (Both laugh explosively)

STARR. (getting down on his knees on one side of MRS. RUST) The greatest show on earth!

JORDAN. (kneeling on her other side) Curtain up!

(They both start to pull up her skirt. ROLAND leaps forward and awkwardly pushes them away from her)

ROLAND. Take your hands off her!

STARR. (gets up. Speaks clear and very menacingly) Get back. Get out of our way.

(JORDAN goes immediately to ROLAND and speaks over his shoulder to STARR)

JORDAN. Now now, Starr. A joke's a joke, but we mustn't upset our friends. Can't you see Mr. Cat's upset?

STARR. (surprised and sincere) Oh is he? I say, I'm

most awfully sorry old man. I wouldn't dream...

JORDAN. Of course you wouldn't. He just didn't see the fun of it, did you Mr. Cat? (Pats ROLAND's arm)

ROLAND. Don't touch me. I don't call that fun. I call it bloody disgusting.

STARR. I see what he means, don't you? A lot of those old Music Hall turns were a bit disgusting.

JORDAN. You're right, they were. And besides he's much too young to remember them. No wonder he was upset. Now Mrs. Rust's not upset, are you Mrs. Rust? (Walks over to her) Mrs. Rust has a real sense of humour you know, a really wonderful sense of humour. So rare nowadays. Dear me, where's your hat?

MR. RUST. (nervous and rapid) Here. It's here. I've got it.

JORDAN. Oh good man. (Takes the hat and puts it carefully back on MRS. RUST) There you are, dear lady. And a very charming hat it is too. Now then, (Walks back to STARR and ROLAND) friends again? That's the way. You mustn't disturb yourself, Mr. Cat...Roland. We progress, we progress. The ways of truth are strange and we must traverse many a twisted and rocky path on our voyage of discovery. We must neither shirk nor evade. Be patient my young friend. Attend. There are crucial discoveries to be made.

ROLAND. But I still don't -

JORDAN. (very earnestly) Of course you don't. How could you? But you will.

(MR. RUST has led his wife back to a bench at the back. She seems calm still. But he is agitated and fusses ineffectively over her, not touching her. Then on JORDAN's speech to ROLAND, he turns and walks over to them)

MR. RUST. And all that - that...I mean what you and...
(Gestures at STARR) were going to my...I suppose
you call...is that what you call 'detachment'?

JORDAN. (bland) No no, we call that 'alienation'. It is a
bit advanced, I confess. It's a rather more subtle
approach.

MR. RUST. To what? Approach to what? I -

JORDAN. People often do have difficulties with it at first.

STARR. (wagging a reproving finger at MR. RUST) I must
say we expected a little more insight from you, sir.
A man of your intelligence...

JORDAN. Perspicuity.

STARR. Perspicacity.

JORDAN. Acuity.

STARR. Prescience.

MRS. RUST. (not moving. She sounds very tired) Leave
him alone.

(There is a pause and JORDAN and STARR look at
each other)

JORDAN. (to STARR) I beg your pardon.

STARR. (turning front) I told them to leave you alone.

JORDAN. (also turning front) I'd be grateful if you'd
refrain from interfering in my affairs. I am not
in need of your protection as it happens.

STARR. I was not protecting you. I was thinking of my
reputation.

JORDAN. That comes rather incongruously from you.
Reputation. Reputation. How funny. What a funny

little thing you are. (Then into STARR's face, smiling, nasty) Who steals my wife steals trash.

STARR. I must say I do find all these quotations and literary references awfully wearing.

JORDAN. (sharp) How is your friend Mr. Cat?

STARR. Mr....? Oh, Roland! I think he must be away. I haven't seen him for ages. Perhaps he's given up... pray heaven.

JORDAN. How do you mean 'given up'?

STARR. Given up pursuing me in that tedious relentless way. You must have noticed.

JORDAN. Noticed? Well of course I noticed. Do you take me for a fool?

STARR. That is neither here nor there. I don't really see what you're getting at.

JORDAN. I'm not getting at anything. It was you who did the getting. You - got - Cat!

STARR. I...got...? (Then is so convulsed with laughter he can hardly speak the next line) You can't mean you thought I was having an affair with Roland!

JORDAN. (nervous bluster) Think? Think? I know.

STARR. (with patronising relish) Then you are a fool... and an ass-head and a coxcomb and a knave, a thin-faced knave, a gull; if you'll pardon the quotation.

JORDAN. I happen to have proof.

STARR. Mr. Know-all is it? Mr. Private Eye?

JORDAN. (gets out small notebook) I have Kept Notes. (Flips through pages) Where were you, for instance, on the night of May the seventeenth?

STARR. If you mean the evening I went to help my niece Ursula with the wedding invitations...

JORDAN. Till five o'clock in the morning?

STARR. Marry in haste. Repent in leisure.

JORDAN. And the night we went out to supper at the Hilton. When you kept getting those telephone calls. Five times you were called away from our table. No explanations. No excuses.

STARR. Goodness did I get it wrong? Is it 'to love honour and obey and explain all phone calls till death do us part'?

JORDAN. You were seen, many times, in the British Museum with Roland Cat.

STARR. As far as I know, fornication is not permitted in the Reading Room... (Then pensive) I <u>could</u> be wrong...

JORDAN. The dentist who you claimed to have visited so frequently <u>does not exist</u>.

STARR. Is there very much more?

JORDAN. Enough for a court of law.

STARR. But so expensive. Perhaps you could just fight Roland. Of course he is stronger...

JORDAN. I would like a statement from you concerning the week when you left home to go to a health farm near Esher and were seen by seven independent witnesses in Boulogne.

STARR. And stupider.

JORDAN. Not to mention the innumerable occasions - I beg your pardon?

STARR. I said 'stupider'. You are neither witty nor wise

but at least you are not a lout. I can only think you know nothing of my nature if you imagine that I might embark on a sexual adventure with a noisy egocentric boy whom I did not like much less love.

ROLAND. Shut up! Shut up! Shut up!

STARR. (very gentle) What did you say, Dodo?

ROLAND. (shocked) Why did you call me that? She always...

STARR. What is it? What's wrong now (Turns to JORDAN) Dodo?

JORDAN. You said you didn't love me. You told your husband you didn't love me.

STARR. Yes I did tell him that.

JORDAN. But you do love me.

STARR. (very reasonable and sweet. A good hostess) Well of course I'm awfully fond of you, Roland.

JORDAN. We were lovers. We are lovers.

STARR. Yes, we did have some awfully jolly times, that's true.

JORDAN. You loved me. You told me I'd made you believe in yourself as a woman. You told me you'd never known what love was before you knew me.

(Now MR. RUST moves quickly back to the mantelpiece and strikes a detached pose)

STARR. Well I don't think I remember saying all that, Roland.

ROLAND. (without appearing aware that he speaks) You did! You did!

STARR. I mean, it doesn't really sound like me, does it?

JORDAN. Why are you doing this? Why are you being like this?

STARR. (stopping and turning to face JORDAN) You're quite sure you want to know?

ROLAND. (under his breath. Very intensely) Yes!

(Now JORDAN turns to ROLAND and gestures deferentially towards him, indicating that he should come and play his part. ROLAND stares uncomprehendingly at him for a moment and then turns suddenly away putting his hands over his ears. JORDAN and STARR look at him, smiling at each other and go on. MRS. RUST seems to have gone to sleep)

STARR. I am 'being like this' as you call it, Roland dear, because I am too tired to 'be like' anything else.

JORDAN. What do you mean?

STARR. Oh I'm so sorry; wasn't that clear? I'll begin again. You bore me, Roland, you bore me entirely.

(By now ROLAND is listening intently again)

JORDAN. You're only saying that because of him being here.

(He points jabbingly at MR. RUST who starts nervously, does a sort of half bow half bob, shoots his cuffs, clears his throat and then turns swiftly round and stares fixedly at himself in the mirror)

STARR. Him? (Laughs) My dear boy, do you think he doesn't know about my lovers?

JORDAN. (in unison. ROLAND jumps to his feet) Lovers?
ROLAND.

STARR. I suppose you thought you were the only one.

(JORDAN looks at ROLAND expectantly. ROLAND

doesn't speak so JORDAN shrugs and goes on)

JORDAN. I know I was!

(Now ROLAND crosses over to MRS. RUST and crouches in front of her, looking up into her sleeping face)

STARR. Don't you remember telling those men when you first came in here about my having 'love affairs all the time'?

JORDAN. I only said that because I was...you know I was only saying it.

STARR. Well that was clever of you, Roland, because it happens to be true. I have had...do have, in fact (Pleasantly surprised after a little mental countup) several lovers.

JORDAN. I don't believe you.

STARR. It is a bit unfair I will admit; after all, they all know about you.

JORDAN. How?

STARR. (sweetly explanatory) We talk about you, you see.

JORDAN. Where? When?

STARR. (lethal) In bed. After.

(There is a pause)

(With a little laugh) One of them... (Looks over questioningly to MR. RUST) I suppose it would be indiscreet to mention his name?

MR. RUST. (very surprised and nervous) Pardon?

STARR. (smiles with brief affection at him then turns back to JORDAN) One of them calls you my little student.

JORDAN. (slumped and stupid) Why?

STARR. (irritated) Because I'm the one...because I teach you. But I'm afraid I'm not a very good teacher. Oh we have laughed together about it. 'He'll never get a diploma, that one' I say. (Laughs)

JORDAN. (defeated) Why do you say that?

STARR. Oh really, Roland. Do I have to spell it out for you? Because you're not very good at it, Dodo.

JORDAN. (muttering, dazed) We were perfect...You always said that. We were perfect together.

STARR. Well of course I would say that. After all, I'm not a monster; I wouldn't want to hurt your feelings. The times I've had to bite my tongue though, not to laugh out loud.

JORDAN. (not a question. A repetition of the word) Laugh.

STARR. (agreeably) And laugh and laugh.

(JORDAN and STARR both turn to look at ROLAND. MRS. RUST is still sleeping)

ROLAND. When we first met it was at a party. I was nervous and upset; drunk too. You stood by the window and you were so still. You looked calm and peaceful. Later you told me that you had been full of despair that night, but you looked safe and sweet to me. I wanted to touch you. You...looked at me. You must have known exactly what I was thinking. You saw me. And then at the end of the evening I just went up to you and I said

JORDAN. (to STARR, flatly) I have a house.

ROLAND. And you smiled and you said

STARR. (as JORDAN. Expressionless) You're too young

to have a house. Why have you got a house?

ROLAND. And then I said...

JORDAN. It's my father's house. But he died on Tuesday. I haven't been back there since, but it's my house now.

ROLAND. And then you nearly touched me. You put your hand out and you said

STARR. You loved your father?

ROLAND. And I said...

JORDAN. I hated him. Come back to my house with me.

ROLAND. And you looked and looked at me, but you didn't say anything so I said...

JORDAN. Please.

ROLAND. And you said...

STARR. Yes.

(There is a strange silence. JORDAN and STARR remain still. For the moment it is clear that ROLAND's piece of truth has made them powerless. ROLAND is staring desperately at MRS. RUST waiting for her to speak but she sleeps on. Suddenly he clasps his head desperately in his hands. His voice is really frightened)

ROLAND. And it was all a lie, wasn't it? It was a lie!

MR. RUST. (with difficulty) No, Roland, no.

(STARR has not moved and seems oblivious of the others but the moment MR. RUST speaks JORDAN pushes STARR almost brutally forward)

JORDAN. (to STARR) Yes Roland yes.

STARR. (precipitately) Yes Roland, yes. And all the time I was thinking to myself 'I've never had anyone as young as this before. Won't it be fun?'

JORDAN. (fast) Fun?

STARR. Yes, fun. Fun and new and exciting and amusing - oh you know. Shall I tell you something, Dodo?

JORDAN. Tell me.

STARR. Every time we made love...if you could call it that...every single time I used to think 'the best thing about this is that it's just like incest! He's my own little baby,' I used to think, 'slobbering and grunting over his Mummy!'

(ROLAND leaps forward and seizes MRS. RUST and throws her onto the floor)

ROLAND. I hate you!

(JORDAN and STARR move back. They exchange one look, one nod. MRS. RUST is moaning. MR. RUST dashed forward when it happened but now stands frozen in embarrassed horror, his hand on his toupee)

MRS. RUST. Roland...

ROLAND. Don't speak to me! I'll kick you! I'll break all your bones! I'll kick your head in!

(He lunges at her and MR. RUST with incredible speed reaches her and pulls her to safety. She covers her face with her arm. MR. RUST holds his own arms curved over her without touching her. When he speaks he speaks only to ROLAND. For the first time it is impossible for him to use, to handle words. He stutters and his face works)

MR. RUST. L...l...l...life...Roland...life!...life!... the temple...body...temple of the soul...remember... sac...sac...sac...sac...

JORDAN. (contemptuous) Sacroiliac? Sacond best? Sakes maniac?

MR. RUST. (forcing the word out. Strong) Sacred!

(JORDAN and STARR laugh. They put their hands out and carefully almost tenderly, they take ROLAND's hands)

Don't...please...you must...Roland...she saw you... you...s...s...s...s...said!...sh...sh...sh... she...s...s...s...s...saw you.

JORDAN.
STARR. (mimicking him) Sssssssssssss! Shhhhhhhhhhh! Ssssssss!

MR. RUST. (singing with great difficulty) Follow follow follow follow follow follow follow me.

JORDAN.
STARR. (in high mocking voices sing back at him) Follow follow follow follow follow follow follow me.

(MR. RUST gets up and goes towards ROLAND. He draws a deep breath before he speaks)

MR. RUST. You understand, Roland, I have always been able to talk very well - on certain minor subjects. I can be remarkably fluent, even eloquent -

STARR. You can say that again!

JORDAN. Talk for us now. Go on - talk. Talk to us about a minor subject. We're loving it, aren't we Roland.

ROLAND. (looks eagerly and nervously from JORDAN to STARR) Yes, loving it.

(Now they draw him back closer towards them)

STARR. He's a scream isn't he Roland?

ROLAND. Yes a scream.

JORDAN. A regular old Punchinello, isn't he?

ROLAND. Yes, yes he is.

STARR. (seized by an odd laughter) Yes, he's Punch and she's Judy and (To ROLAND) you're the baby and we (Almost can't get it out for laughter) we're the crocodile.

JORDAN. (low but sharp to STARR) Watch it.

STARR. (angry) What do you mean, watch it?

JORDAN. What I say. This is crucial.

STARR. (very edgy) I know it's crucial. You don't have to tell me that.

JORDAN. We won't get the woman.

STARR. I know that.

JORDAN. But we've got this one. Get that one.

MR. RUST. (with ferocious control) There are two ways, Roland, only two real ways...D...d...danger in both...risk, yes. But only in one of the ways is e...e...e...e...

JORDAN. E...e...e...e...e...
STARR.

MR. RUST. (through their voices. Very loud) Evil! (Then pants with the effort) Do you understand me Roland?

ROLAND. (loud and mocking) No!

JORDAN. Help the gentleman, Starr. He can't get it right. Besides, he's exhausted.

(He pushes STARR forward and now holds both of

ROLAND's hands himself)

MR. RUST. The two ways...the two ways...

STARR. Are the winning way and the losing way.

MR. RUST. (moves to STARR hopefully but dubiously) Yes...yes...and in order to -

STARR. In order to win you must briefly consider the milkman whom I may have mentioned earlier.

MR. RUST. (despair) No! No! No!

STARR. (tense. Gabbling this rather) Simply concentrate on this simple analogy and the whole question becomes simplicity itself. I have my toupee, the milkman has his hat. I have my wife, the milkman his horse. His horse weighs considerably more than my wife, but on the other hand his horse talks considerably less. I have not infrequently let my mind dwell on the possibility of suggesting an exchange to the milkman.

(JORDAN and ROLAND laugh but STARR's eyes are closed in concentration)

MR. RUST. (urgent and close to STARR but not touching him) You know what I want to say to him.

STARR. (his teeth clenched) Leave me alone. (Then he opens his eyes, shakes his head and speaks very fast) There are those, for example, who maintain that the milkman's horse is happy pulling his heavy load. This is untrue. Horses have feelings too. A man's best horse is his friend. After all, people are -

MR. RUST. (interrupting. Very strong) Alone!

STARR. (after a pause. His head hangs down and he speaks unwillingly but compelled with pain and a sort of sickness) And afraid. Poor fools!

JORDAN. (decisive) Starr!

(STARR looks at him and then backs away)

(Turning to ROLAND) We've heard enough of this rubbish haven't we, my friend? We'd better be off.

(ROLAND nods confusedly and they move towards the door)

MR. RUST. Wait...wait! Roland...1...1...listen to me... Listen! (He speaks jerkily and hits himself when he gets a word wrong) She told you...I heard...I heard... It was right...<u>Partakes</u>...she said that...the image and likeness of...you <u>heard</u>...celebration...yes... and outside the safe place...jackals Roland! (Points wildly at JORDAN then at STARR) Crocodiles!...he said...he <u>said</u>!

JORDAN. He's raving poor fellow. Not surprising. Wife like that. Poor chap, eh? Poor chap. Come along... my son. (Then matter of factly to STARR) Shall we go?

STARR. No! (Then with hatred) Keep the quarry yourself.

ROLAND. (half laughing to JORDAN) What does he mean - quarry?

(After a moment's pause, JORDAN deliberately and violently pushes ROLAND away. ROLAND falls onto his knees and in a panic crawls over to MRS. RUST)

JORDAN. (calmly to STARR) I thought this might happen.

STARR. You know <u>everything</u>.

JORDAN. (businesslike) No more than you. You know that these are only scum.

STARR. (exhausted) But essential to us.

JORDAN. (mild) Raw material. Nothing more.

STARR. Something more. We cannot manage without them.

JORDAN. (nods. He is still very calm and patient but quite without emotion) Which gives them some value. Otherwise they are worthless - corrupt, sluggish and fraudulent. They are as gross and trivial as maggots. They breed and swarm, lust, raven and mutilate; you know all this. The weak ones die in putrefying heaps all over their world. But the rest of them go on jigging and buzzing as usual. Or they pick away at their monotonous little scabs or hide their pig faces in their hands and whine. They are nothing. Filth.

STARR. (with real passion) And that's what we feed on!

JORDAN. (after regarding him for a moment) I'm going. Are you coming with me?

STARR. (turns savagely on the others) We're going. Are you coming with us? (The RUSTS and ROLAND draw close and huddle together) You might as well. All of you. It's what you really want. Evasion and unwisdom and lies - destruction. It's not the dark you're afraid of. Come with us. We're the Technicians. It's simple. We displace all the needs and deform all the reasons. It's what you want us to do. You make it so easy for us - we hardly have to lie to you; most of what we show you is true or could be. You can't get enough of your own truth into your mouths to stop you longing to be victims. You're afraid but you're glad too. No one blames the victim. He (Nods towards JORDAN) he's right about you. I don't pity you! Don't think I pity you! Cowardly - fatuous - neglectful - fools! You run to us begging us to destroy you. No. You shuffle. That's it - you shuffle into our trap sweaty and naked and weeping with relief!

(Now a train whistles like a scream. Then silence. JORDAN goes to the door and opens it. He looks back at STARR)

JORDAN. You're finished Starr. It's over. (He goes)

STARR. Yes! (Then as he begins slowly to fall, his voice

is peaceful) Yes. Yes. Yes. Yes.

(MR. RUST clumsily catches him as he falls. The light fades to a spot on them. MR. RUST takes off his toupee and holds it absurdly over his heart. He is quite bald)

CURTAIN

STAY WHERE YOU ARE

STAY WHERE YOU ARE was first performed at The
Traverse Theatre Club, Edinburgh, on 28th December, 1969,
with the following cast:

NINA	Antonia Pemberton
ELLEN	Louise Breslin
TADDY	Ian White
DAVID	Michael Harrigan

The play was directed by Michael Meacham.

(The stage is dark. There is the sound of footsteps outside)

ELLEN. Are you all right? Be careful.

NINA. You be careful with that bag. (We hear her fumbling with the key in the lock) Swinging it about. There's breakables in that bag. Bloody key. (Wails) There! I've dropped it now. I've dropped my key.

ELLEN. Wait. I'll get it. Here it is. Shall I do it?

NINA. Do dear. There's a good girl.

(The door is opened and the light from the street shows us a Basement flat, near slum, cluttered, dank, smelly. They come in. NINA is a fat old woman in her seventies, derelict looking, spectacles, a knitted hat. ELLEN, about thirty, is pretty and well dressed. NINA leans heavily on a stick and ELLEN helps her through the door)

ELLEN. Well, if you're all right now. Oh. Your bag. (Puts it down) I'll have to go.

(NINA puts her head back and makes a noise between a howl and a groan)

(Very startled) What is it?

NINA. The pain's come back. Me leg. I've got a blood clot under me knee.

ELLEN. Here. Sit down.

NINA. (sits with ELLEN's help) Oh...that's better. That's a bit better. Turn on that light. (ELLEN looks about) Over there!

(ELLEN does. NINA rocks back and forth in the chair, holding her leg and groaning. ELLEN stands watching her aghast. Eventually NINA stops rocking and is silent, eyes closed)

ELLEN. (after a pause. Just touching her) Are you all right?

NINA. The pain's gone off now. (But she doesn't open her eyes)

ELLEN. Well...I'm awfully sorry but I really have to be going.

NINA. (opening her eyes and turning her head slowly to look at ELLEN) Going? How am I to manage?

ELLEN. (childish) I have to go. I was waiting for someone when I saw you. He'll be there now.

NINA. Stuck here in this chair. I won't be able to move for a hour now. I know that. I get these attacks. I know them.

ELLEN. He'll think I'm not coming.

NINA. (indignant. Reproachful) I've only been out of hospital three days.

ELLEN. But isn't there somebody here? To take care of you?

NINA. Who - him? I have to cry like a baby before he'll take me up to the toilet.

ELLEN. Your husband?

NINA. I wouldn't have him for a husband. He's not right.

ELLEN. Does he live here?

NINA. He lives here all right. Oh yes, he lives here.

ELLEN. Well he'll be back soon won't he?

NINA. Who knows? Stays out all night sometimes. (Piteous) All on my own here. Can't move. No one to protect me and the pain so bad sometimes I cry out in prayer I can tell you.

ELLEN. (more childish but more desperate) I have to go.

NINA. Make us a cup of tea first, eh? Will you just make a cup of tea for a poor rubbishy old woman?

ELLEN. But he won't know where I am.

NINA. Your husband is it?

ELLEN. (brief pause) Yes.

NINA. Well he'll wait. He'll wait for his pretty wife.

ELLEN. No I must go. He'll be worried.

NINA. But you're not worried about me, are you? Oh no. Help an old woman across the road. That's right. That's a good deed. Didn't want to help me back here though did you? You'd have left me there. Got me across the road and just left me. What's the good of that? I had to beg for it. There's your good Samaritan.

ELLEN. Well why were you out? You shouldn't have been out at all.

NINA. Someone had to get some food didn't they? He's brought nothing in. Perish from hunger - he wouldn't care. It's took me hours just to get down to that little shop across the road. People going past making out I was drunk. That's what they think if you're poor. 'Oh, she's drunk' they say. 'What a frightful old woman. Look at her,' they say. Never think you're just out of hospital. Nearly died. I won't last long, I know that.

ELLEN. Oh you will...I'm sure...

(NINA looks straight at her and ELLEN trails off. There is a silence and then NINA laughs)

NINA. It'd be easier for you if I'd popped off before you ever seen me. And he'd be glad. He'd be ever so glad to come home and find I'd popped off. (She pauses) And I don't know nobody else.

ELLEN. Nobody?

NINA. Nobody. (Leans forward and speaks slowly) I'd like a cup of tea.

ELLEN. (after a pause) Where's the kettle?

NINA. (leans back. Closes her eyes) It's behind that curtain. (Waves her arm towards it) All the comforts of home. Sink, gas ring - we'll need a bob or a sixpence. Got a tanner my duck?

ELLEN. I think I've got a shilling. Yes.

NINA. Meter's under the sink.

(ELLEN goes behind the curtain. We hear her fill the kettle, put the shilling in the meter and light the gas. Meanwhile NINA has with difficulty taken off one shoe, pulled her skirt up and peeled down one stocking. She starts to unwind a dirty elastic bandage from her leg)

(Calls) I say. Ducky.

(ELLEN comes out)

Give us a hand with this bandage dear, will you, while the kettle's boiling.

(ELLEN walks slowly towards her)

(Struggling with it) I'm too weak, that's all. Got to be done twice a day, see. (ELLEN sits on her heels and starts gingerly to unwind the bandage and roll it up) Has to be tight to stop this clot moving up to my heart. That's it. That's got it.

(ELLEN has wound up the bandage. She gets up with it it in her hand)

Now put it back on again. (ELLEN crouches down again) No not like that. You got to start it right up here. (She pulls her skirt even further up) Right round here. That's right. Move over a bit dear. Then I can rest my foot on your knee there. That's the way. That's better.

(She puts one hand on ELLEN's shoulder as she rewinds the bandage, her leg stretched out straight, the foot resting on ELLEN's lap)

(Crooning it) That's it. Right round. Round again. Nice and tight.

(The door opens quietly so that they don't hear it. A man, TADDY stands in the doorway watching them. He is in his fifties with grey hair but a youthful face. He's wearing a tattered greatcoat and sucking a lollipop)

TADDY. (takes the lollipop out of his mouth and makes a sweeping gesture) Mother - and - Child.

(ELLEN cries out, startled)

NINA. Mind out! (Looks round) Oh it's you. (Then to ELLEN) It's only Taddy. Finish it off then. There's a pin on the end. Not so fast. Ow - oh - oh - ow - not so fast!

(ELLEN finishes and putting NINA's foot on the floor she gets up)

(Querulous) What about my stocking?

TADDY. (strides briskly over) I'll do that.

(Holding the lollipop in his mouth he puts on her stocking and her shoe. Then he takes the lollipop out of his mouth and holds it up to NINA)

Suck?

NINA. No, I want my tea. (Throws lollipop across the room)

ELLEN. (who has been edging over to the door) The kettle's boiling - in there. (To NINA) You'll be all right now won't you. Your - he'll get you some tea.

TADDY. Oh no. She won't let me make the tea. Not when somebody else is here. Hates my tea.

ELLEN. But I'm just going.

TADDY. (very reasonable) Well, you can make the tea before you go.

ELLEN. (helplessly) Please...

TADDY. (over his shoulder to NINA) What's she doing here?

NINA. (offhand) How do I know?

ELLEN. I - I just helped you up the road! (To TADDY) She didn't seem to be able to walk. I don't think she ought to be out so soon after being in hospital.

TADDY. (friendly, scathing) She wasn't in hospital.

ELLEN. Oh.

NINA. (mild. Matter of fact) I was.

TADDY. (casual) All right, you were.

ELLEN. Well...goodbye.

TADDY. (craning round to look at ELLEN) Why don't you just make her some tea.

ELLEN. But you're here now. You can do it.

(TADDY goes over to the bed and lies on it his arms crossed under his head)

TADDY. I could. But I'm not going to.

ELLEN. Why? Why not?

TADDY. Because I don't want to. (Brief pause) You don't want to either.

ELLEN. But I don't live here. I don't even know her.

TADDY. You have to know people before you can make them a cup of tea?

ELLEN. That isn't fair.

TADDY. Did you want to help her home?

ELLEN. (miserable. Very young) I don't know.

TADDY. Why did you do it then?

ELLEN. I don't know.

TADDY. You must have had some reason. Felt sorry for her?

ELLEN. Yes - yes I did.

NINA. Sorry enough to see me across the road. Not sorry enough to get me home.

ELLEN. I did bring you home. I put the kettle on. I did your bandage.

NINA. Yes but you didn't want to. I had to make you didn't I?

(TADDY sits up and pats the end of the bed)

TADDY. Here.

ELLEN. What?

TADDY. Come and sit here.

ELLEN. No!

NINA. (closing her eyes) Don't be naughty dear. Do as you're told.

TADDY. (still patting the bed. Speaks gently but firmly) Come here.

(ELLEN comes over but doesn't sit. Stands looking down at him)

(Shrugs) Now. Try and think. Why did you help her across the road?

ELLEN. (mutters) Because I couldn't think of any way out of it.

TADDY. (warm) Very good. That's very good.

NINA. (sits still with eyes closed) That kettle will be boiling its liver out.

TADDY. And why did you bring her home?

ELLEN. She wouldn't let go of my hand.

TADDY. And then you put the kettle on.

ELLEN. Yes.

TADDY. And then you did her bandage.

ELLEN. Yes.

TADDY. Why?

ELLEN. She _told_ me to.

TADDY. And you always do as you're told. (Pause. Then raps it out) Make the tea.

   (They look at each other. Then ELLEN turns and runs to the door)

ELLEN. I won't. I don't have to. (Pulls at the door handle)

NINA. (surprised) You going?

ELLEN. Yes! I didn't want to come here in the first place. You never thanked me; that doesn't matter. But I did help you even though I didn't much want to. You can't make me stay here.

   (TADDY rises and walks over to her and stands with his back to the door. She backs away from him nervously)

TADDY. (points to the curtained kitchen, his eyes steadily on ELLEN) Get in there and make the tea, do you hear me?

   (As if by reflex ELLEN turns and starts for the kitchen. TADDY and NINA roar with laughter and she stops and looks at them)

ELLEN. (scared) Why are you laughing?

NINA. Talk about a monkey on a string!

TADDY. (smiling and shaking his head) You _do_ do what you're told. Well, well. Amazing.

NINA. (banging her stick on the floor with great violence) Tea! I want my tea! I want my tea!

TADDY. (not looking at her) Stop that.

   (NINA subsides into mumbling. ELLEN looks from one to the other, starts to speak, then changes her mind and walks with artificial purposefulness to the door)

(Genuine surprise) Now what?

ELLEN. (firmly) I must go. I have to meet (Stumbles slightly over the words) my husband. Would you let me by please.

TADDY. (who has shifted slightly to block the door again) Oh come on. It's not your husband - now is it?

ELLEN. I - I - I - I - don't know what you mean.

TADDY. There's no need to pretend. We've known all along. (Goes over to NINA and stands beside her) Haven't we, Nina?

NINA. (largely) Well a course we have.

ELLEN. Known what?

TADDY. You must have thought we were very naive. She must have thought we were just a couple of old fuddy duddies eh, Nina?

NINA. Stick-in-the-muds. (Pause. Thoughtful) Sticks-in-the-mud.

TADDY. (his hand on NINA's shoulder. The Victorian father. Grave and pompous) Now we don't want to give you advice. Heaven knows you should be old enough now to make your own decisions. But there is one thing I'd like to say. Just one last word. I think we're agreed on this point my dear? (Looks down enquiringly at NINA. Her attention has wandered and she is picking her teeth. Now quickly folds her hands in her lap and nods at him) We'd just like you to reflect a little about family life. The protection of the young. The little lives which have been put into your care. The home. The nest... (Points at ELLEN in sad accusation) How many innocent people will suffer - answer me that!

NINA. (regretful head shaking) He's right, dear. It wouldn't be fair. Poor little pretties - it wouldn't be right.

ELLEN. (sort of half laughs) You're both mad. I <u>mean</u>. Insane.

(They look at her steadily)

TADDY. (gently) How many children has he got - two is it?

ELLEN. (shocked) How -

TADDY. (raps it out) And you've got three haven't you?

ELLEN. (automatic. Staring at him) Yes.

TADDY. (reasonable. Smiling) Well, that's five for a start isn't it - to suffer I mean. Not to speak of the other wife and other husband of course. Seven.

NINA. (warmly pleading) Oh don't forget the grannies, dear. Don't leave them out. They'll be heartbroken. (Clicks tongue and looks sadly at ELLEN)

TADDY. (rueful) A good deal of pain, I'm afraid.

NINA. And the grand-dads a course (Getting quite involved and counting on her fingers) Not to mention the uncles and aunties. And the cousins there would be -

TADDY. (firm) That'll do. (Then light and mild) I'll go and make that tea now. (Goes at once)

(ELLEN has been standing frozen through this. Now she watches TADDY go and after a pause she goes quickly over to NINA. We hear TADDY whistling in the kitchen)

ELLEN. Is he a detective?

NINA. <u>I</u> don't know.

ELLEN. You said - you said he came in at all sorts of hours. (Absurdly methodical) Does he have a tape recorder?

NINA. (snapping her fingers. A bit exaggerated) Yes! He does! You could be right. He never tells me nothing.

ELLEN. No, it can't be. (Firm) It's too silly.

NINA. Expect you're right. Silly. Yes. (Pause) Still - it's funny. Your saying that I mean. For example, sometimes he'll go out with this other bloke - a photographer he is - and they always go ever so late at night and most times he don't get back here till morning.

ELLEN. A photographer!

NINA. That's right.

ELLEN. Oh God. I suppose he could be -

NINA. Well, he could. I mean it would hang together wouldn't it.

ELLEN. I don't know - I don't know......Maybe it would make it worse to go now. I don't know. Do you think I should stay?

NINA. You must do as you think fit, my dear. I wouldn't like to advise.

ELLEN. But it's such an impossible coincidence. How can he know anything about me? He couldn't know I was coming here. I mean, I'm only here by accident - (Breaks off and stares at NINA. At this point TADDY's whistling in the kitchen stops abruptly)

NINA. (sweet, enquiring) Yes dear? Go on.

ELLEN. (puzzled. Not believing this but knowing it) You brought me here. You did it all on purpose.

NINA. (bit dangerous) Oh I see. He sent me out to fetch you is that right? (ELLEN is silent) Is that what happened? (Still no answer. Then in a strong cruel tone) Eh?

ELLEN. (brave) Yes. Yes I do think that happened. It all fits in.

NINA. (more dangerous) Fits in. Oh yes. (Very sweet voice) And where does my leg fit in? You'd say there's nothing wrong with it would you? (ELLEN nods) All part of the act, eh? (ELLEN nods again)

NINA. It's all about you isn't it? The story's always got to be about you. (Brief pause. Then spits it out with pain and venom) Selfish little bitch! (Closes her eyes, puts her head back and speaks privately) I was in hospital. I was the one lying in bed awake all night waiting for that clot to get up to my heart. Sweating and crying - all alone. Nurses - cheeky hard-bitten little madams. Doctor doesn't even look at you. Just a useless heap of rubbish nobody cares about. (Opens eyes and looks clearly at ELLEN) Nor do I care, mind. Just enough to stay alive.

(TADDY has come through again unseen by them and has been listening)

TADDY. (gently contemptuous) You were not in hospital.

(ELLEN starts and stares at him. NINA doesn't move. Pause)

NINA. (throwing her stick violently across the room) Oh all right!

ELLEN. You weren't! (Then to TADDY) She wasn't! None of that was true. There's nothing the matter with her!

TADDY. (lighthearted. Grinning) Oh I don't think I'd say that.

NINA. (bitter) Oh very funny and witty I'm sure.

ELLEN. (effort at calm) Before I go, I would like some kind of explanation. I think - I think -

TADDY. Yes?

ELLEN. (rather quavering dignity) I think you may both regret all this - regret it very much.

NINA. (looking at her with admiration and even affection) Well! Well then! Ah...it's a shame. (Then to TADDY) And where's my bloody tea?

TADDY. (Irish) Now aren't I the great ninny? (Bustles out and comes in again with the tray) Tea is served, gentlemen. (Then own voice) Keep a cup hot for me in the pot. I'm just going up to make a couple of phone calls.

(He goes out another door)

NINA. (pouring) Milk and sugar dear?

ELLEN. (rapid) I don't want any. Calling who? Who's he telephoning?

NINA. (generously regretful) How would I know, dear. How would I ever know? Here. You take this tea. (Proffers cup) It's good and strong and it's good and sweet. You're looking very peaky. (ELLEN automatically takes the cup) There's my duck. Go on now - sit down. (ELLEN goes. Takes a swig of her own tea) Ah, that's good. (Looks over at ELLEN who is just holding her cup and staring at nothing) Drink it up old lady.

ELLEN. (puts cup on floor. Very childish voice) I don't want it.

NINA. (squinting at her) Well poor mite. (Shouts towards the door TADDY left by) Poor mite I say! (Then looks at ELLEN, puts her head forward and nods confidentially) Here. Don't believe all I say when he's here, eh?

ELLEN. (suspicious) What do you mean?

NINA. I got no home of my own you know. Nowhere to go

but here. No Visible Means of Support.

ELLEN. (whispers) Do you mean he pays you?

NINA. Pays me! All you young people think about is money. (Looks at ELLEN and speaks quite matter of factly but not without sympathy) You don't understand nothing do you?

ELLEN. (loud. Desperate) No! No I don't! (Puts her face in her hands and sobs) I don't know what to do!

(NINA watches her in silence for a little while she weeps. Then holding her cup in her lap, she sings softly)

NINA.
    Warm hands warm
    The men have gone to plough
    If you want to warm your hands
    Warm your hands now.

(ELLEN looks up at NINA through her fingers)

(Grins) My gran used to sing me that. Nice isn't it?

    Warm hands warm
    The men have gone to plough
    If you want to -
(Breaks off and speaks briskly) Tell you what we'll do.

ELLEN. (wiping tears off her face with her fingers) What?

NINA. Now where's that stick?

(ELLEN looks around vaguely, not seeing)

Never you mind. I'll get it.

(She heaves herself off her chair and starts to crawl grotesquely in the direction of the stick, grunting and puffing. ELLEN gets up and backs away staring at her, horrified)

ELLEN. But you said you hadn't been in hospital.

NINA. (briefly. Over her shoulder) He said.

    (ELLEN starts to go forward to help her but NINA waves her away)

    Never mind. Never mind. I'm used to this. Go and listen at that door. See if he's coming back.

    (ELLEN goes over to the door and puts her ear to it)

ELLEN. (whispering) I can't hear anything.

NINA. (getting herself up to a standing position with the stick) Ups a daisy! (Looks shrewdly over at ELLEN) He thinks he knows everything. (Pause. Nods) There's a lot he doesn't know. (Pause) For one thing he is jealous! Now that is one thing I am not. My Dad used to say to me, 'Nina, there is not a jealous bone in your body.' (Then to ELLEN) What's your name?

ELLEN. Ellen.

NINA. Hmm. Bit plain. Elaine would have been nicer. More style. What did your daddy call you?

ELLEN. El. He always called me El.

NINA. Don't think much of that. I'll call you Elaine.

ELLEN. Please...

NINA. Don't rush me dearie. You think old Nina's just rambling on. But all the time (Taps her forehead) I'm thinking. I'm planning.

ELLEN. Planning what? Are you going to help me?

NINA. (rolling her eyes) Well a course I'm going to help you, silly little juggins.

ELLEN. Will you tell me what to do? Can I go? (Starts

to cry again) I want to go and find - (Breaks off)

NINA. Find who?

ELLEN. (not looking at her) M-m-my husband.

NINA. Oh now. There's no use starting that again is there? I told you before. Jealous! Taddy! He's jealous!

ELLEN. (utterly puzzled) But you don't mean he's jealous of me.

NINA. Oh Elaine, Elaine. Oh deary deary deary. We shall never get on at this rate. Here. Sit down will you? I can't get on with my planning - you standing about like a scared rabbit.

(ELLEN sits in the chair)

Now you just listen to Nina. When he comes back - the minute he comes in - I want you to faint! Flat on the floor!

ELLEN. Why?

NINA. (kind/irritable) Because I say so.

ELLEN. I can't. I don't think I can.

NINA. Course you can. Course you can. Easy enough. Just keel over. Any fool can do that. I'd show you myself if it wasn't for this sodding stick. All right then. There you are - stretched out. That'll stop him. 'It's the shock' I'll say (Dramatic delivery) 'She may never recover from this' I'll say.

ELLEN. Then what will happen?

NINA. 'Fetch a doctor, quick!' I'll say. Then (Pause) While he's out of the way, up you get and off you run safe home to beddybyes.

ELLEN. But how can I go? He knows things about me. (She

stands, her hands over her mouth staring at NINA) He's a blackmailer!

NINA. Shhhhhh! I didn't say it. (Low) Now you listen to me, Elaine. He knows nothing. He never saw you before tonight. It was me picked you.

ELLEN. But why did you do it? Why?

NINA. (reproving Nanny) Try and think of others, Elaine dear. I got to do what I'm told or it would be the old heave ho for Nina. Tipped out in the street.

ELLEN. (painfully trying to work it out) Do you mean you just go out...I mean he sends you...to choose someone ...anybody...and then frighten them about some secret they might have.

NINA. Everybody's got secrets, duck, and I must say you weren't much cop at hiding yours. Candy from a baby with you. That's why I felt sorry for you.

ELLEN. (turns away) You say you're sorry for me. I don't believe you.

NINA. (sad) Don't then. I can see as how you wouldn't.

ELLEN. (turns back and looks at her) You really will help me?

NINA. (licks her finger, draws it across her throat and holds it up) Promise!

ELLEN. (going right up to her. Nearly touching) I do believe you.

NINA. (puts her hand on ELLEN's head) There's my good girl. Now - the minute we hear him coming, over you go. Can you do that?

ELLEN. Yes I can. I'll do it.

NINA. That's right. I knew you could. You stay here and

I'll be by the door. You watch me for the signal.
Right?

ELLEN. (nods. A little excited now) Right.

(NINA goes over to the door. ELLEN watches her, hugging herself and trembling a little)

NINA. (looks over at her and smiles) Don't worry, then. It'll be all right. Don't you worry.

(ELLEN manages a smile and NINA nods and smiles back)

(ear to door) Nothing yet. Not a sound. (Straightens) Do you know? I get a funny sort of dream sometimes. Well it's not really a dream because I'm awake. Like just before I get up out of bed in the mornings or like before I drop off at night. I get this feeling they've taken off the top of my head. Doesn't hurt or anything. It's just gone and I feel all lovely and empty, and then I can feel this sort of <u>growing</u> right inside my head. It's growing up and up and I stay ever so still. Flowers. All growing out of the top of my head. Lilacs and honeysuckle and daffs and bluebells - all sorts. There's this lovely sweet smell and I can feel the flowers hanging down and brushing against my face - just rustling like against my ears and my eyes. (She smiles to herself. Then looks over at ELLEN and grins) You think I'm daft.

ELLEN. (quickly) No I don't. I don't.

(They wait. Then there is the sound of footsteps)

NINA. He's coming. Quick! Now!

(ELLEN looks wildly about and then awkwardly and in a panic throws herself face down on the floor)

(loud) Oh my God! Oh my God!

(Holding her stick under her arm she runs very lightly

over to ELLEN. Kneels beside her. The door opens. TADDY comes in followed by a young man, DAVID. They go over to NINA and ELLEN)

TADDY. What have you done to her?

NINA. Me! What did I do? She's just had a fit or something that's all. You've scared her into convulsions that's what you've done.

DAVID. Oh Jesus! Ellen.

(He tries to get to her but TADDY neatly intervenes. ELLEN pulls herself up to her hands and knees and looks unbelieving at DAVID)

ELLEN. David! It's David! Oh you're here. You're here. How did you find me?

DAVID. (to TADDY) I'll go and get some brandy.

TADDY. Right. (DAVID goes quickly)

ELLEN. (after a blank silence) He's gone.

TADDY. He'll be back. (Then businesslike) Nina. Go and wash up these tea things. And find a glass in there.

NINA. (cheerful) Right-oh Taddy. Right-oh, right-oh right oh (Puts her stick down, collects the cup and waltzes out with the tray) Anything to oblige. Mind your backs ladies and gentlemen please. (When she gets through the curtain she starts to sing) 'She was a sweet little dicky-bird, tweet tweet tweet she went' -

TADDY. (raising his voice slightly but not looking in her direction) All right.

NINA. (sticks her head through the curtain) Spoilsport! Isn't he a mean old spoilsport, Elaine?

TADDY. (flat) Nina.

NINA. (sulky) Oh all right. (Goes)

ELLEN. She is crazy.

TADDY. Yes. Now what about this fit of yours?

ELLEN. It wasn't - I mean I didn't. She told me to.

TADDY. Ah. I should have known that.

>(He folds his arms and puts his head back and stands quite still, eyes closed. Then drops his arms, opens his eyes and looks at ELLEN)

>You know - sometimes it gets to be a bit too much for me. It really does.

ELLEN. What does?

TADDY. (rubbing his eyes with the heel of his palms) I'm tired. (Looks at ELLEN again) I can't always know the right thing to do, can I?

ELLEN. I don't know.

TADDY. You say that a lot don't you.

>(ELLEN doesn't answer)

TADDY. (bit impatient) You'll have to do some of this. I can't do it all.

ELLEN. Some of what?

TADDY. After all, you've got responsibility for it too.

ELLEN. How? What do you mean? Who for?

TADDY. (exasperated) Well for Nina, for example. You came here with her.

ELLEN. Yes but I didn't want to.

TADDY. (sighs) I'm talking about what you did, not what you felt. (Then begins walking about speaking more or less to himself) Well now what. What's for the best I wonder. I wonder.

ELLEN. He'll come back and he'll take me away.

TADDY. Possibly, possibly. Let's wait and see about that, shall we? It's not, after all, the main issue.

ELLEN. It is for me! I want to go.

TADDY. (reasonable) We all <u>always</u> want to go. Does it occur to you that this might be hard for me too? And for Nina - God knows. No, I can see that it wouldn't.

ELLEN. You said she was crazy. She is.

TADDY. Yes yes.

ELLEN. And...and...and I think you are too.

TADDY. (genial) A possibility not to be discounted. And you - what about you? (Laughs kindly) Throwing yourself on the floor? Pretending to have a fit?

ELLEN. I didn't <u>want</u> to do that.

TADDY. But you had to because she told you to. Another one of your little sayings.

(DAVID comes in. ELLEN jumps up and goes to him)

DAVID. (to ELLEN) Are you all right?

ELLEN. Yes. Can we go now?

TADDY. (friendly, apologetic) I'm afraid it was all Nina's idea - one of her famous charades. (To ELLEN) And you went along with it. Very generous.

ELLEN. (to DAVID) Can we go?

(NINA comes through the curtain, a cloth shopping bag over her head)

NINA. Come on Tad. Marco! Marco!

(TADDY gives an elaborate rueful shrug to the others and goes up to NINA)

TADDY. Polo!

(She lunges and he moves quickly out of the way. He motions the others to join in)

NINA. Marco!

DAVID. (moving towards her and grinning back at ELLEN) Polo!

NINA. I'll get you! (Lunges. Misses) Marco!

TADDY. (quick) Polo!

NINA. Marco!

DAVID. Polo! Come on Ellen.

(NINA has been going towards one and then the other. Now comes straight for ELLEN)

NINA. Marco!

ELLEN. (fast. Nervous) Polo!

(She doesn't move and TADDY darts back and moves her out of NINA's path)

NINA. Marco!

TADDY. Polo!

NINA. Marco!

DAVID. Polo!

(ELLEN runs over and stands by him. He puts an arm around her)

NINA. Marco!

DAVID. (to ELLEN) Go on.

ELLEN. (bit braver) Polo!

(NINA moves in fast. DAVID shoves ELLEN aside and NINA gets him. She pulls the bag off her head)

NINA. Ha! ha ha. (Dances him round and then gives him a rather long slobbery kiss. Looks over her shoulder at ELLEN) Don't mind do you dear? I did win.

TADDY. That's the only reason she plays this game. For the kissing. Great slut!

NINA. (delighted) Who you calling a slut?

TADDY. (friendly) You. You're a great slut and a fat sow.

NINA. Oh naughty. Personal remark. (To others) That's right isn't it? Personal remark - bad manners. (Then to TADDY) Weasel!

TADDY. Walrus!

NINA. Cheat. Cheat. Walruses are men. Snake!

TADDY. Snakes are women.

DAVID. (loud and sudden) Wait! Stop! I can hear something outside. Turn out the lights.

(TADDY immediately does)

ELLEN. (whisper) What is it? David where are you? What is it?

DAVID. Shhhhh! Don't know yet. Wait.

(Silence)

NINA. (quavering) It's not them again Taddy. It's not them is it?

TADDY. (tense, clipped) Don't think so. Don't be frightened, Nina.

NINA. Hold my hand Taddy. You know I can't stand being alone in the dark.

TADDY. Here. I'm here. Be quiet now. Shall I go and have a look?

DAVID. No. Stay where you are. I'll go.

ELLEN. David don't go! Please don't go!

DAVID. It's all right. Just stand quite still.

(We hear him going over to the door)

NINA. (muttering it rapidly) Soul of Christ sanctify me. Body of Christ save me. Blood of Christ intoxicate me. Water from the side of Christ wash me. Passion of Christ strengthen me. Oh good Jesus hear me. Within thy wounds hide me. Never let me be separated from thee. From the malignant enemy defend me. At my death call me and bid me come to thee that with thy saints I may praise thee forever and ever Amen.

TADDY. Amen.

(Silence again)

DAVID. (loud. Cheerful) All clear! Let's have the lights.

TADDY. (turns on the lights) Phew! What we all need now is a drink.

ELLEN. (to DAVID) Who was it? What was it?

TADDY. Nobody this time, thank God. Where are these

glasses, Nina?

NINA. There's only one, Taddy. (Brings out half pint mug)

TADDY. Well, we'll just have to have a loving cup. (Holds glass out to DAVID who pours brandy into it. Then hands it to ELLEN. Very courtly) Our guest first.

DAVID. Drink Ellen. It'll do you good.

TADDY. That's it. (Then hands it to DAVID but NINA intervenes and grabs it)

NINA. Ladies first. (Drinks)

TADDY. Nina nina. You're supposed to be the hostess.

NINA. (to DAVID handing him the glass) Sorry ducky.

DAVID. Quite all right. Well. Here's to the good life. (Drinks and hands it on to TADDY)

TADDY. (raising glass) The Good Life. Champagne and Cadillacs and a month in the country!

ELLEN. (goes up to DAVID and whispers) Please can we go now?

DAVID. Hang on, love.

ELLEN. (whispering) But why can't we?

NINA. Whisper, whisper (Wags her finger) Bad manners again.

DAVID. She's a bit upset.

NINA. I'm not surprised, poor little Elaine. Frightened into a fit like that. I don't wonder. Oh it's a man's world, my dear. Take it from me.

TADDY. She didn't <u>have</u> a fit.

NINA. There now, there I go again. Mixing things up. It's

the shock. Have some more brandy, Elaine lovey.

TADDY. That's right. Come and sit down. (Pours some more and leads her to a chair. Then to DAVID) She's trembling.

(DAVID goes and sits by ELLEN on the floor. He puts his arm across her legs and hugs them)

DAVID. It's all right. It's all right.

(ELLEN drinks and NINA comes over and takes the glass)

NINA. Better now? I know how you feel. It's hard on a woman. (Moves about orating and drinking) Night after night I'll sit here - sometimes without no light if I haven't got a tanner. Oh and I hate the dark. I'll just sit waiting - waiting. Him out (Indicating TADDY) God knows where - larking about. And I think to myself, 'Nina' I think, 'This could be the night.' Knock on the door. In they'll come. Break the door down most likely - I wouldn't open it. Paralysed with fear in my chair waiting for it to happen. Crash! (ELLEN jumps and NINA pats her and says softly) Crash. In they'd come. There they'd be. 'Your turn, Missus! (Dramatic thrilling tones) It's your turn now!'

TADDY. You always think it's your turn, Nina. Why should it be you? Bet you thought it was your turn tonight.

NINA. Might have been. Might have been. Why not I'd like to know?

TADDY. It might have been mine. Or his. (Pause) Or hers.

(Silence and they all look at ELLEN)

ELLEN. My turn for what? (To DAVID) What do they mean?

NINA. (through laughter to TADDY) She thought you were

a detective.

(DAVID and TADDY laugh heartily)

ELLEN. She said you were a blackmailer.

NINA. Oooooh I never. What a fib. I didn't, Taddy. (To ELLEN) That was your story.

DAVID. (kind. To ELLEN) Really? Did you really think that?

ELLEN. I didn't know what to think. I didn't understand what was happening.

TADDY. (to the others) Be fair. It's not surprising. (To ELLEN, smiling) Everything happening so fast. Not a bit surprising.

NINA. I couldn't tell her could I, Taddy? I mean I couldn't tell her all about you. It wouldn't have been right.

TADDY. (formal. Grave) No, that's true, Nina. It would not have been right and I thank you for your discretion.

NINA. (humble) Thank you, Taddy. But you could tell her, couldn't you.

TADDY. (looks down. Pensive. Then looks up) Yes. Yes. I could tell her.

NINA. (pulls up a chair near ELLEN and sits down) Taddy'll tell you.

TADDY. (mannered and actorish but not parody) It's a sad little story and rather stupid. I was a doctor - quite a good doctor in fact. When I was forty, something happened to me. (Deprecatory) I won't say it was the Voice of God. (Serious again) But I did feel I'd been - well - called. I suppose you could say it was a sort of vocation - mission - something like that. I left my home.

NINA. Muswell Hill.

TADDY. (shoots her a brief glance. Then nods and smiles reminiscently) Muswell Hill. (Then very seriously to ELLEN) I left my wife and children. I left my excellent practice - the whole life I'd known and loved. And I went down the East End of London. To the worst slummiest part of the docks. I wanted to live with the Meths drinkers. I felt I could help them to... find their way back. (Pauses)

DAVID. (respectful) What happened?

TADDY. (shrugs. Ironic) What happened was that my capacity for suffering, my zeal for combating the ugliness and waste turned out to be less than my sense of personal despair. The despair being, I suppose, why I went into the absurd bloody thing in the first place.

DAVID. (sympathetic) I suppose so.

TADDY. (jaunty) Well, I cracked up all over the shop, became an alcoholic myself and ended up far worse than those people I'd gone out to 'spend my compassion' on. They had none for me. They hated me. (Turns away, moved) I couldn't run. I didn't know where to run to. Or why. So I tried suicide. A pathetic attempt. (Turns back) Nina found me. (Simply) She saved my life. (NINA smiles and shakes her head, looks down at her hands) We came here.

DAVID. (after a pause) And now you look after her.

TADDY. That's about it. I do what I can. One to one salvation. (To ELLEN) How does that sound to you?

(She looks into TADDY's face. The other two look at her)

ELLEN. I - I'm sorry.

(NINA and DAVID exchange a very faint smile)

TADDY. Ah, don't be sorry for me. I'm safe here. Nina's safe.

NINA. You never know, Taddy, you never know. The knock on the door.

TADDY. No, you never do know. It's best not to forget. (To DAVID) You understand that I think.

DAVID. Yes I think I do. (Shakes his head) It's uncanny. (Looks up at them) Do you know - my own father died when I was thirteen - a hopeless alcoholic.

NINA. (warm) Funny old world.

ELLEN. (to DAVID) You never told me that.

DAVID. I've never told anyone, Ellen, until just now. And I could never forgive my father either. But now, somehow, I think I do forgive him.

NINA. That's right. God rest him. We're all sinners dear. All miserable sinners.

DAVID. I'd worshipped him, you see. I was the only child and I thought he was the most wonderful man in the world.

NINA. (leaning forward) And what was your Mummy like, dear? It must have been terrible for her.

(DAVID, as TADDY did, looks at her briefly)

DAVID. My mother?...Oh she (Laughs fondly) was a beautiful foolish woman. I never took her very seriously, I'm afraid. All she seemed to care about was parties and pretty clothes. I hadn't any idea, you see, that she was just putting up a front on a hideous situation. She kept it from me. Then - when - when it happened...Oh, I don't want to bore you with all that.

TADDY. No no, please. I think you should tell us.

NINA. What did she do, poor thing?

DAVID. Well there was no money of course. She just went out to work. She didn't know how to do anything really. Jobs in shops, working in a laundry, dishwashing - Oh, she'd always lose the job but she just went on - on to another and another. She so desperately wanted me to stay in school and have a career. But... she just wasn't strong enough. (Pause) She couldn't take it.

ELLEN. (taking his hand) Did she... die?

(Now TADDY and NINA exchange the same faint smile)

DAVID. No. She didn't die. She's... in an asylum not far from Eastbourne.

TADDY. Do you see her?

DAVID. Oh yes. Once a week I go down there. She lives in a kind of dream really. Sometimes I wonder why I go. You see she doesn't know who I am.

NINA. Doesn't recognise you - her own son?

DAVID. No. (Pause) Sometimes she thinks I'm my Father. (Pause) Those are the worst times.

(There is a silence)

NINA. Oh what a tragedy. What a sad and tragical story. It reminds me. Oh it has taken me back; just all that about the pretty clothes. I had such lovely clothes once. In Paris (To ELLEN) if you could believe that.

TADDY. No she couldn't.

NINA. Why not pray?

(ELLEN takes her hand from DAVID. Touches NINA's knee)

ELLEN. Go on. Go on. Please tell me.

NINA. (sulky) You heard what he said.

ELLEN. (urgent) No. I didn't. I didn't. What were you doing in Paris? Tell me.

TADDY. 'Ran away from home at sixteen?' 'Artist's model in the Latin Quarter?' It's a hopeless ridiculous story, Nina, and you know it.

NINA. I don't see why? What about him trying to shoot me on that Channel Steamer?

ELLEN. Who? Who did? Tell me.

NINA. The painter chappie, dear, what I lived with.

TADDY. Oh give over Nina. We can't take all that.

NINA. (triumphantly indignant) See! Spoilsport again! We can take your story. Oh of course. Oh definitely. Doctor in Muswell Hill indeed.

TADDY. You said Muswell Hill.

NINA. Well I was a bit cross. Naturally I was thinking it was going to be the one about you being a master in that public school and caught in bed with one of the boys. All the scandal and the disgrace. (Aside to ELLEN) I was the school cook, see.

ELLEN. No. No. No. No. No.

TADDY. That's where that one falls to bits. You a cook. You can't even make a cup of tea.

NINA. I could.

TADDY. Yes you could. But you won't and you don't. (Then to DAVID) How is your mother?

ELLEN. Don't!

DAVID. Wonderful for her age, really. She and my father

have a cottage in the country. He's retired now.

(ELLEN puts her hands over her eyes and doubles up, hiding her face in her lap. DAVID gets up and moves away and they all three stand looking at her. There is a silence)

NINA. Got a pain perhaps.

TADDY. Looks more frightened to me.

DAVID. I expect both.

NINA. I get a pain in my tum when I'm frightened. (Brightly) No need to be scared Elaine dear.

(ELLEN sits up and looks at them all)

ELLEN. I'm not Elaine. I'm Ellen. Ellen. Ellen.

DAVID. Yes?

(A pause while she stares at him)

ELLEN. That's all (Hugs herself tight)

TADDY. Well, it's quite a lot.

(Another pause while they regard her)

NINA. (judicious) She is frightened you know. Look at her. Like a little wild creature in a trap.

DAVID. (kindly) Well actually that's one of her favourite parts. She's extremely good at that one.

NINA. Oh - is she an actress? Are you an actress, duck?

DAVID. (still pleasant) More of a performer really.

(ELLEN stares at him with real pain and then convulsively doubles up again)

DAVID. (strong and sharp) Don't do that! Sit up!

(Slowly ELLEN does but she can't look at him)

NINA. Well there's no need to shout, surely. Poor little poppet. You're not to shout at her. (Claps her hands) I tell you what - we'll have another little game. That'll cheer her up. Hide and seek. (To ELLEN) You can he 'It' first. (Then louder to her) Hide and seek, dear. Quick now. We're only going to count to twenty.

(She claps her hands over her eyes. TADDY and DAVID follow suit. NINA starts counting and they join her and all count louder and faster to twenty. ELLEN just sits absolutely still, staring)

Ready or not, here we come!

(They uncover their eyes and start looking elaborately and silently round the room under things and behind things)

DAVID. Nobody found her yet?

NINA. Not a sausage.

TADDY. She's very good at this - remarkable.

NINA. Well where can she be?

ELLEN. (sudden. Wildly) I'm here!

(They all turn round and look at her astonished and delighted)

NINA. There she is!

TADDY. Well you certainly had us fooled.

NINA. (to DAVID) Your turn now, dear.

(She and TADDY put their hands over their eyes. They have counted to five when NINA takes her hands down and looks at ELLEN)

Oh naughty. Mustn't cheat. (Goes over to her and puts her hands over her eyes for her) No peeking now. Back to one, Taddy. We weren't ready. One!

(And again she and TADDY count faster and louder to twenty)

TADDY. Ready or not here we come!

(They take their hands down. DAVID has moved to sit directly in front of ELLEN on his heels. Her hands are still over her eyes. TADDY and NINA start looking round the room again)

NINA. (turning and looking at ELLEN) Oh now. Who's being naughty again. Play up, play up and play the game. Open your eyes.

TADDY. (goes over to ELLEN and takes her hands down) You've got to look too.

NINA. We can't find him anywhere.

ELLEN. He's here! He's here!

NINA. There now. She's found him.

TADDY. Very quick. Very quick indeed. This girl's a champion, Nina.

(ELLEN looks into DAVID's face and speaks with real entreaty)

ELLEN. David?

(He looks impassively back at her. She gets up quickly and backs away. At once DAVID gets up and steps back to join the others)

DAVID. Something wrong?

ELLEN. Don't speak to me! You're one of them.

DAVID. And who are 'they'?

ELLEN. (pointing) Them! Them! They're the ones who made me come here.

TADDY. (quiet but a little dangerous) Made? Made? How 'made'?

NINA. Who started it then? Who began?

ELLEN. You did!

NINA. Oh no, you came up to me. You began.

ELLEN. You kept me. You wouldn't let me go.

DAVID. (sharp) Forced you?

ELLEN. I didn't say that -

TADDY. Locked all the doors did we?

ELLEN. No, it wasn't -

DAVID. Are you saying you've been kept a prisoner here?

ELLEN. (loud and desperate) No! No! No!

(There is a pause)

NINA. (comfortably) Well a' course she wasn't.

TADDY. (laughs gently) A prisoner...dear, dear, dear.

DAVID. (to ELLEN. Clinical and interested) You are frightened.

ELLEN. Yes.

DAVID. What of?

ELLEN. You all told lies. All of you. You just go on telling lies.

NINA. Stories more, really.

ELLEN. And games. And turning off the lights. And something bad outside only nothing really. Pretending not to see when you could. Another lie or a game or a joke. Nothing ordinary. Nothing real.

TADDY. If it's not ordinary it can't be real?

NINA. No surprises, eh?

ELLEN. It's not that. I don't mean that.

DAVID. What do you mean?

ELLEN. (haltingly to him but emphatic too) I mean you have to understand things. You have to know what to expect. You have to know what's going to happen, what to do.

DAVID. (with real feeling. To her) No! No! You don't!

ELLEN. I do.

DAVID. Why? You tell me why, Ellen.

ELLEN. Because...because if everybody breaks all the rules then - then it all falls apart.

TADDY. What rules?

ELLEN. (to DAVID) You know. Everybody knows. The rules about what you ought to do.

NINA. And what you oughtn't?

ELLEN. Yes! Yes! I broke the rules (To DAVID) and I'm being punished for it now. I knew, I knew all along I'd be punished for it.

(There is a pause and then TADDY goes over to her.
He speaks directly to her with a gentle intensity)

TADDY. Listen. There was once an old woman who lived in
a little house facing a mountain. Now in order to get to
church, which she did every day, she had to cross over
the mountain. She was old and she was tired. One day
she was reading her bible and she came across the bit
that says faith can move mountains. And she thought to
herself, 'well,' she thought. So that night she closed
her little chintz curtains and she sat up the whole night
through praying that the mountain would be moved.
When morning came, she drew the curtains and there
was the mountain. And she looked, and she said, 'I
knew He wouldn't.'

(Silence. NINA and DAVID make a slight movement
forward. ELLEN looks from one to the other)

ELLEN. (turns away) I don't understand. I don't understand.

(DAVID steps swiftly forward, takes her by the
shoulders and turns her round to look at him)

DAVID. (angry and desperate) No of course you don't.
How could you? Ellen, that story's about you. That's
what you do. Can't you see? If you find you can't plan
and decide ahead and make sure everybody, including
you, plays the parts you've given them, you just stop
being anyone at all. You can't control the situation so
then you believe that the situation is controlling you.
Then it all has to be a conspiracy, you the victim.
Either way - either way, Ellen, nothing is allowed to
occur.

ELLEN. (defiant. Releasing herself from his grasp) And
does everyone have to be mad before anything can
occur?

DAVID. (turning away. Wearily) Maybe. Yes. Probably.
Up to a point.

ELLEN. It isn't like that. It can't be like that.

DAVID. (facing her again) It isn't like anything. It just is. (Puts his hands on top of his head, frustrated. Then takes his hands down and speaks fast) Look, look. I'll show you what you would have wanted all this to be like. (Goes over to NINA) What were you doing when she came up to you. Go on. Show me.

NINA. I wasn't doing nothing. Just standing there leaning on my stick. (Starts to act this as she goes on) Oh yes, that's right, I did get a bit cross. All them bleeding cars. None of them would stop for me. Rush rush rush, back and forth. So I starts shaking my stick and shouting a bit. 'Bastards! Stop will you! Let me across one of you buggers!'

DAVID. Well that would be wrong for a start. (To ELLEN) That's wrong isn't it? Poor old ladies don't swear. (To NINA) Just be helpless and pitiful. I'm her coming up to help you.

(Takes a few steps away and then walks back looking solicitous)

NINA. Oh, oh what shall I do? I'll never get home. Won't somebody help a poor old woman?

DAVID. Can I help?

NINA. Oh would you, Sir - Miss, I mean. God bless you Miss.

(They act crossing the street)

DAVID. Are you sure you're all right? Can you get home by yourself?

NINA. I'll manage. Don't you worry your pretty little head about me. It's only just up the hill.

DAVID. I'll see you home. No, it's no trouble. Here, take my arm.

(They walk a few more steps. Then TADDY comes forward and mimes, opening a door)

TADDY. Oh there you are, Mother.

NINA. (indignant) Mother!

TADDY. (smothly) Shut up Nina. I was getting quite worried about you, Mother. You know you didn't ought to be out on your own.

NINA. This young lady seen me home.

TADDY. There's kind. Please do step in, Miss. Now Mother you come and sit down. (He and DAVID sit her down) She's not been out of hospital long, you know.

NINA. (shivering) I'm cold, <u>son</u>. I'm cold. Put the fire on.

TADDY. I've got no money for the meter, Mother. I'll get you a blanket.

DAVID. Please. I've got plenty of sixpences and shillings in my purse. Take them, do.

TADDY. Oh you're too kind. She's too kind isn't she, Mother?

NINA. Ah, you don't meet many Christian people these days.

TADDY. At least let us give you a cup of tea.

DAVID. No no. I must go. (And then with a kind of smiling savagery) I've 'done' you two, you see, and now I've got to go and 'do' him.

(Now, slowly, TADDY and DAVID turn to look at ELLEN. She looks back. Then she gets up violently from her chair knocking it over deliberately)

ELLEN. (calm) I hate this place.

> (She starts to move round the room, methodically turning over chairs and tables, pulling pictures off the walls etc. She is silent, concentrated and swift. The others just watch her attentively)

There! (She looks round at the mess) I did that!

TADDY. Yes.

NINA. Why?

DAVID. Were you angry?

ELLEN. (with glad rage. Loud) Yes!

DAVID. (nice, loving laugh) Good. Good. Good.

ELLEN. (to him. Ferocious and loving) You can go to hell!

> (She picks up her bag and walks straight out the door. The others stand still for a moment)

NINA. She's left the door open. (Looks at DAVID) Aren't you going after her, dear?

DAVID. Yes.

NINA. That's right. That's right, isn't it Taddy?

TADDY. Yes.

CURTAIN

JACK THE GIANT-KILLER

CHARACTERS

JACK

THE EXAMINER

FATHER

MOTHER

(Lights up on bare stage. One man, the EXAMINER, sits in a wooden swivel chair. He is in morning coat, etc, sits with his legs crossed and is holding a bound folder open on his lap. Seated cross legged on the floor a few feet in front of the EXAMINER with his back to him is JACK, about twenty, long hair, jeans, army surplus greatcoat. Not a hippy or a dropout. There is a silence. Then the EXAMINER yawns politely)

EXAMINER. We're wasting Time.

JACK. Maybe for you. Not for me.

EXAMINER. On the contrary. The time is not, in any case, mine at all.

JACK. You mean you don't care what happens. You're not interested.

EXAMINER. What 'happens' is to you. Not to me.

JACK. You're not concerned then.

EXAMINER. Not personally, no.

JACK. (speaking rather violently) Well I am.

EXAMINER. Inevitably.

JACK. (after a pause) What do they call you anyway?

EXAMINER. The Examiner.

JACK. (laughs) You're the one who decides whether I pass or fail.

EXAMINER. The question of success or failure doesn't come into it. There are certain alternatives. You choose one.

JACK. Or none.

EXAMINER. That is one of the alternatives.

JACK. (half exasperated, half joke) Bloody Jesuit you are.

EXAMINER. (amused) Hardly. Shall I have them sent in?

JACK. (jumping up) No! No, not yet - I'm not ready.

(The EXAMINER settles back in his chair. Folds his hands)

(Pacing around) I mean - it's all right for you. You haven't got to decide anything, have you?

EXAMINER. (patient) No.

JACK. It's not easy this.

(The EXAMINER says nothing)

(Facing him. A bit angry) It's hard! It's very hard!

EXAMINER. (gently but dry) Yes. Very hard.

JACK. (sitting down again rather suddenly, putting his face in his hands) Besides I don't understand it.

EXAMINER. Scarcely anyone does. Before, at any rate.

JACK. (looking up at him) You mean I will understand - after?

EXAMINER. (kind but as always a little impersonal) I
   hope so.

JACK. (letting out his breath in a sort of long sigh) All
   right. You can let them come in.

   (The EXAMINER rings a small bell. He leans back
   again. Folds his hands. JACK looks nervously about.
   Then we hear voices and footsteps. The MOTHER and
   FATHER enter from the back. We hear their voices
   before we see them. As soon as JACK hears them he
   moves on his bottom pushing himself over to the
   EXAMINER where he sits with his back as it were
   against the wall. He looks very tense and apprehensive)

MOTHER. (voice off) Stuck in there - we've been waiting
   in that poky little room fully twenty minutes. I think
   it's outrageous. You should have said something,
   Father.

   (The FATHER says something indistinguishable)

   (Irritable) What? What? I can't hear a word you're
   saying.

FATHER. (exasperated) I said 'Say something to who?
   There was nobody there.'

MOTHER. (as they come on) Always muttering. You and
   Jack both. Never speak up either of you.

   (They come on. Lower middle class. MOTHER wears
   a coat with a fur collar and a downright looking felt
   hat. FATHER wears best suit, probably only suit, and
   a bow tie and spectacles)

   (Stopping as she sees JACK. Speaks crossly) Oh there
   you are Jack.

JACK. (jerks) Yes.

MOTHER. Well what is the meaning of all this? Dragging
   us here, keeping us hanging about. The message said

'urgent'. Your father's very angry.

JACK. Hello Dad.

FATHER. Hello Son.

MOTHER. You don't say hello to me though do you? Oh no, of course not. Just a simple courtesy to your own mother -

EXAMINER. (interrupting but not rudely. Gestures to the three empty chairs) Please. Sit down.

(His voice is authoritative enough to silence the MOTHER and the two parents go over to the chair and sit down. The EXAMINER opens his folder, runs his finger down a column)

(Looking up) There is a sister?

MOTHER. (promptly) She couldn't come. She's working for her 'O' Levels.

(FATHER mutters something again)

EXAMINER. I beg your pardon?

MOTHER. (triumphant) There you are. No one can hear you. It's not only me, you know.

FATHER. (very clearly) I said 'you wouldn't let her come'.

MOTHER. Let! That girl makes up her own mind believe you me. Besides it's none of her affair all this - this - I see no reason why she should be dragged into it.

JACK. I'd have liked her to come. Biddy.

MOTHER. Oh yes, of course you would. The two of you! Always conniving together. Secrets. Her name is Bridget. How many times do I have to tell you?

JACK. (stubborn) I'd have liked her to come.

MOTHER. Well she didn't want to.

FATHER. She did.

MOTHER. And besides it wasn't suitable.

EXAMINER. Pardon me.

(They all look at him)

We have not got a great deal of time. There are others waiting. Biddy is not, for whatever reason, here. May we proceed?

FATHER. (loud and sudden) Yes! For Christ's sake! Let's get on.

MOTHER. (shocked) Father! Language!

EXAMINER. (smiling very nicely at the FATHER and speaking gently) Yes. For Christ's sake.

(He picks up the bell and this time rings it loud and long. Immediately two figures run in and up onto the platform where they stand stock still facing the EXAMINER. They both wear half masks, neutral. The MAN has a beard and is dressed in overalls. He carries a doll wrapped in a blanket. The WOMAN has long grey hair. She is dressed in a blue robe)

The Mother.

(The MOTHER figure turns and bows)

The Father.

(The FATHER figure turns and bows)

The child.

(The FATHER figures raises the doll over his head

in both his hands)

Please begin.

(Now backstage there is the sound of a hand drum beaten rhythmically but not very loud and a recorder playing. The sound should be rather oriental and strange. The FATHER figure puts the doll gently on the floor in front of JACK. Then he and the MOTHER figure put their arms round each other very tenderly and stand still for a moment. Then the FATHER figure goes over and gets the doll. He goes down on one knee in front of the MOTHER figure and gives her the doll. She holds it to her breast and circles slowly round where she stands, her face up showing joy. The FATHER figure goes and puts his arms round both the MOTHER figure and the doll and they dance a slow dance of celebration. Then the music stops. They stand still. Silence. Then a sudden sharp roll of beats on the drum. The MOTHER figure pushes the FATHER figure away and turning her back on him rocks and sways bending over the doll. Twice the FATHER figure tries to get in front of her to make her look at him, to touch the baby. Each time she turns sharply away. The FATHER figure crouches on the floor grieving. The MOTHER figure stands still, her back to him, holding the baby in her arms. Silence. Again the sudden sharp beat of drums. The FATHER figure leaps up and tears the doll from her. She wrenches it back from him. Four times they pull the baby from one to the other. The last time the doll splits in half and each is left holding one half. The recorder gives a high note like a scream. Silence. The two figures turn and kneel facing JACK. They put the two halves of the doll down before him. JACK pulls back from them, scared. He looks wildly at the EXAMINER)

JACK. What am I supposed to do?

EXAMINER. What you want to do.

(JACK inches a little closer to the doll. Looks down at it)

JACK. (puzzled sad voice) Poor baby. (Then imploringly to the two figures) Why'd you do <u>that</u>?

(They don't answer)

(Looking down again) Poor baby. Poor little bugger. (Very tenderly he picks it up and fits the two parts together as well as he can and wraps it in its blanket) There you are, mate. There you are. You'll be okay. (And he holds the doll rocking it slightly)

(Now the drum beats loud regular rather military beats. JACK looks up startled)

(To EXAMINER) What's that for? What's going to happen now?

(The EXAMINER reaches behind his chair and brings out a wooden prop sword. He proffers it to JACK. The two figures rise and backing away from JACK stand still and put their hands behind their backs still facing JACK)

(Frightened) What's that? I don't want it. Why should I want it? Take it away.

(The EXAMINER still holds out the sword and JACK, clutching the doll to him stares at him horrified)

I won't take it! I don't have to!

EXAMINER. No. You don't have to. You can give them back the baby.

JACK. I won't. They don't deserve it. They tried to kill it. Somebody ought to kill them. (He stops abruptly and then repeats very slowly) Somebody ought to kill them.

(He and the EXAMINER look at each other. Then JACK puts the baby down very gently. He takes the sword and stands up. He moves towards the MOTHER figure)

MOTHER. Jack! Put that silly sword down at once do you hear me? What do you think you're doing? These people are all insane. I won't have you joining in with them - making a fool of yourself. Haven't you any self-respect? And what about me? What do you think I feel like? What would people say if they could see me here - see my son acting like some kind of a lunatic. (JACK slowly raises the sword) Jack! I am speaking to you. Do as your mother tells you. Jack!

(And he stabs the MOTHER figure who falls silently at his feet, the MOTHER begins to weep and JACK turns to the FATHER figure)

FATHER. (clears his throat) Son?...... Your mother's right, son. These people are all nutters. Look how upset she is. You've made your mother cry. Be a good lad, Jack. Come home with us now......Son?

(And JACK stabs the FATHER figure who falls at his feet. JACK lets the sword fall and stands quite still his eyes closed, his face calm)

EXAMINER. And Jesus said....

JACK. (clear and peaceful. Eyes still closed) Before Abraham was, I am.

EXAMINER. And the Prophet, Kahill Gibran said.....

JACK. He said: Your children are not your children. They are the sons and daughters of Life's longing for itself. They come through you but not from you. And although they are with you yet they belong not to you. You may give them your love but not your thoughts, for they have their own thoughts. You may house their bodies but not their souls. For their souls dwell in the house of tomorrow which you cannot visit, even in your dreams. You may strive to be like them, but seek not to make them like you. For life goes not backward nor tarries with yesterday. You are the bows from which your children as living arrows are sent forth. The archer sees the mark upon the path of the infinite, and He bends you with His might that His arrows may go swift and far. Let your bending in the Archer's hand be for gladness; For even as he loves the arrow that flies, so He loves also the bow that is stable.

(Now JACK opens his eyes and looks at his parents. Both have their faces in their hands)

EXAMINER. Go to them.

(JACK steps over the body of the figures and goes to his MOTHER, raises her up and kisses her gently)

JACK. Goodbye Mum.

(She stands looking at him as he goes to his FATHER and raises him up. He hugs his FATHER)

Goodbye Dad.

(Now the two figures rise, the FATHER figure picks up the doll. They bow to the EXAMINER and to JACK and his parents. Then they go)

(To EXAMINER) Can I go now?

EXAMINER. (matter of fact) Oh yes. If you're free to go.

JACK. (indicating his parents) Will they be okay?

EXAMINER. They'll manage.

JACK. Hey - wait a minute. What about Biddy?

EXAMINER. There will be a time for her too. There is a time for everyone if they can take it.

(Then JACK hugs himself hard and looks up at the ceiling and smiles)

JACK. (exultant. Half laughing) Oh boy! Oh boy!

(Then he drops his arms, waves at his parents, gives the thumbs up to the EXAMINER and starts to go)

Tara all (Then to his parents) I'll keep in touch. Be seeing you.

(And he runs off. His parents watch him go, then turn and look at each other. The FATHER puts his arm round the MOTHER and leads her off the stage and out.

The EXAMINER watches them go. Then closes the book, puts it on the floor and picks up another one like it. He rings the bell as the lights dim out to darkness)

CURTAIN

NEITHER HERE NOR THERE

CHARACTERS

BOY

ALICE

BETTY

KAY

MARILYN

LUCY

GIRL

MATRON

DOTTY

(Dim lights up on a very bare room. There is a
candle burning on a box in the corner. There is a
small table and one plain chair. The stage is silent
for a little. Then there is the sound of a sort of muffled
groaning or howling in the distance. It gets louder and
louder and with it there are the sounds of several pairs
of feet and scuffling noises. The only voice is the
moaning one. Suddenly the door is flung open and a
BOY is hurled onto the floor in the middle of the
stage. He is dressed Jackie Coogan style, flat cap,
trousers with suspenders, striped shirt, jacket etc.
The others follow him in, five of them dressed in
grey capes and gendarme-like hats. They look like
Eastern European traffic police. One of them closes
the door and stays by it. The others come in and
stand round the BOY. He lies face down on the floor,
his legs drawn up, his arms clasped around his head.
He shudders and whimpers. They are silent except
that they all breathe deeply from the effort of dragging
him. However this breathing is exaggerated and too
regular. It gradually becomes more and more regular
and louder until it is like a menacing drumbeat
composed of breath. As this continues the BOY
becomes absolutely still. Then one of the people
stamps a foot sharply and immediately the breathing
stops. After a slight pause the person speaks
commandingly in a very deep voice and an extremely
pronounced foreign accent)

No. I. Sit up you!

(Immediately the BOY sits up. He keeps his hands
over his face and looks through his fingers from one

to another of them, terrified)

Chair!

(One of the others goes swiftly over and gets the chair and places it centre stage facing out. The BOY looks at it, puts his hands down and starts to move away from it pushing himself along on his bottom)

NO. II. (Again very foreign accent. Gruff, rather disgusting voice) Shall we strip him?

NOS. III, IV, V. (at once. Hissing it very lasciviously) Yes!

NO. I. (lazily) Not yet. No.

(Now the BOY has begun to move more round the room. Nobody tries to stop him. He gets into a sort of crouch-crawling posture and moves quite fast whimpering again. They regard him as they talk)

(Stretches and yawns) We will talk to him. Tie him up - yes?

OTHERS. (as before) Yes!

NO. I. Hurt him a little.

OTHERS. Yes!

NO. II. (hard) He must be punished.

NO. III. (sharp whisper) Tell us his secrets!

NO. IV. He will never leave this place alive.

NO. V. (flat. Practical) No. We will deal with him tonight.

(All this time the BOY has been moving more frantically round the room. No one has moved to stop him. From time to time they move out of his way almost courteously. Now he is over in the corner and suddenly he blows out the candle. The stage is dark at once. We hear the BOY sobbing and panting and his running feet. Then he screams)

NO. I. (immediately after the scream) Light!

(And a spotlight goes on beamed down onto the centre chair. The BOY has been caught at the door by NO. V who holds him by the arms. His arms are outstretched, head down on his chest. The four others are standing in pairs downstage backs to the audience facing the chair)

Now we tie him. Clearly he is impatient to begin.

(NO. V brings the BOY to the chair. Two of the others get ropes and tie him to it. He sits head down, submissive. They circle slowly round him)

(As they move) Your name?

(He doesn't answer)

NO. II. Your name!

NO. III. Your name!

NO. IV. Your name!

NO. V. Your name!

(He remains silent)

NO. I. The chain.

(One of them goes and gets a vicious looking chain)

The whip.

(Another gets a little whip. They continue to circle during this)

Now! (They all stop moving at once. She speaks very strongly and slowly) Tell us your name.

(He remains quite still and silent. Doesn't look up. They all take a step or two forward. There is a menacing silence)

(In a girl's voice) All right don't then. Mine's Betty.

(And she takes off her hat letting her long hair fall loose)

BOY. (looks up astonished) Wh - wh-wh-what?

NO. II. Mine's Alice. (Takes her hat off)

(Others take hats off. Smile at BOY)

NO. III. Mine's Lucy.

NO. IV. Mine's Marilyn.

NO. V. Mine's Kay.

BOY. (looking from one to the other) But why? Why? You must all be crazy!

ALICE. (hard and strong) No we are not! (Pause. Smile) We're just bored.

BETTY. And terribly frustrated. You know? (Smiles. Then to the others) This one is rather yummy isn't he?

ALICE. I bet he's dirty. He smells.

MARILYN. I think that's nice.

KAY. You would. You really revolt me you know that?

MARILYN. Good. From you that's a compliment.

KAY. (looks at her briefly. Then speaks to the BOY)

How old are you anyway?

BOY. Seventeen.

(They all make delighted noises and comments: 'Great' 'That's divine' 'Just right' etc.)

BETTY. See, I told you. I don't know why you guys don't listen to me every time.

LUCY. Because it wouldn't be fair, Betty. We all get to take turns choosing.

BETTY. Yeah. Yeah. Sure. And look what happened when it was your turn.

LUCY. Well it wasn't really my fault. I mean he was so tall and everything -

BETTY. Twelve years old! I mean! We are not in the pre-puberty stakes.

LUCY. And he was smoking...

ALICE. So what does that mean? I started smoking when I was ten.

MARILYN. And being tall hasn't got anything to do with it. This one isn't very tall.

BETTY. No, but he's the wiry type.

KAY. And, boy, is he ever strong! I'm telling you I could hardly hold him over there. (Nods toward door)

MARILYN. Oh goody. I can't wait. Let's get started.

BOY. What do you mean 'started'?

ALICE. We don't even know his name yet. What's your name?

MARILYN. Who cares about his name. Let's go. Let's go. Let's go.

LUCY. Well I want to know his name. And I think he has a right to know a little bit about what's going to happen to him. I mean, heavens, how would we like it if we were in his position.

MARILYN. I would love it.

LUCY. I was not addressing my remarks to you, Marilyn.

BETTY. Lucy's right. (Then genially to the BOY) The thing is this is a pretty awful place to live in and it's even worse because we're all girls, but we have to stay here -

BOY. Why?

BETTY. (sharp) What?

BOY. Why do you 'have' to stay here?

BETTY. (angry) None of your business.

KAY. (fierce) We ask the questions, buddy, not you.

MARILYN. What did I tell you? (To BOY) Why don't you just shut up whatever your name is and do what you're told.

BOY. I don't have to take orders from you.

MARILYN. Oh no? What makes you think that?

BOY. I'm not afraid of a bunch of girls.

ALICE. Well if you aren't now, angel, you soon will be.

LUCY. Oh Alice, that sounds so mean.

BOY. (writhing against the ropes) What are you going to do to me?

LUCY. See? You've got him all upset again.

MARILYN. So what? Why don't you just shut your trap, Lucy.

LUCY. (affronted) Well pardon me for living.

MARILYN. I'm not about to pardon you for living. Go ask God if that's what you want.

KAY. Will you quit, Marilyn.

MARILYN. Well she's so dumb!

ALICE. We're all of us crippled in our different ways, Marilyn dear.

KAY. At this rate we won't have time to do anything.

BOY. (desperate) Do what? What do you mean?

KAY. (kindly) Gosh, you're stupid, aren't you. Didn't you even hear what Betty said?

BOY. (sullen) No. Who's Betty?

BETTY. (stepping forward. Very gracious. Enunciates crisply) I am Betty and what I said was that we are all very frustrated.

ALICE. Do we have to spell it out to you?

LUCY. (rather motherly) You see, that's why we brought you here. What we do is we all take turns.

MARILYN. We all take turns and we do exactly what we feel like doing. And what I feel like doing (Steps forward and starts to unbutton his jacket) is to get some of your clothes - Judas Priest! It's a girl!

(The GIRL puts her hands over her breasts and cowers away)

ALICE. (snatching off the GIRL's cap) You little bitch!

LUCY. (shocked) What a cheater!

KAY. Where's that whip...

(They all close in and crowd round the GIRL. She is terrified and shrinks from them)

GIRL. Don't! Please don't hurt me! I had to dress like this. It's a disguise. I've just escaped from a mental hospital.

(There is a pause and they all stare at her. Suddenly BETTY starts irrepressibly to giggle and then they all laugh nicely and stroll away from the chair)

BETTY. That is really a good one. I bet you wish it was true.

(LUCY and ALICE go over and untie the GIRL)

GIRL. (irritable) I don't know why you always have to be so rough, Marilyn. Who are you anyway - Tarzan? You've torn my shirt.

KAY. Never mind, Dotty honey. Next time it'll be Marilyn's turn.

(A bell rings in the distance)

BETTY. My God, there's the bell. She'll be here in a few minutes. (Starts hurriedly taking off her cape. The others do too)

LUCY. (scared) Oh come on! Hurry! You know what she's like today.

ALICE. She's like that every day.

KAY. No, I agree with Lucy. She's getting worse all the time. For God's sake, Dotty, get those pants <u>off</u>!

(They are all getting their capes off, picking up the hats
and putting everything into the box in the corner.
Underneath they are wearing shirts like DOTTY's and
plain blue skirts rather long, black shoes)

BETTY. Here's your skirt, Dotty. (Throws it to her and
DOTTY throws back the trousers etc. which KAY
puts in the box)

Put the other light on, somebody.

(ALICE goes over and switches off the spot and turns on
another light. The stage is now lit in a strong cold
rather bluish light)

LUCY. What shall we play? What shall we play? I'm sure
I can hear her coming.

MARILYN. Red Rover. That ought to be childish enough
for her.

(They form two lines of three facing each other on
either side of the stage. MARILYN, BETTY, ALICE
in one and DOTTY, KAY, LUCY in the other)

Red Rover, Red Rover, let Kay come over.

(KAY lets go of the others' hands and runs across and
tries to break through the line. She tries to get through
MARILYN and BETTY's hands but she can't and falls)

KAY. (to MARILYN) God damn you, Marilyn, that hurt.

MARILYN. (very sweetly) Oh <u>I'm</u> sorry, Kay.

(KAY now links hands with BETTY)

BETTY. Red Rover, Red Rover, let Dotty come over.

(DOTTY comes over very fast and breaks through
MARILYN and ALICE's hands)

MARILYN. (loud) Ouch! Hell! (nurses her wrist) You've

just about broken my wrist, you little creep.

DOTTY. (over her shoulder, strolling away) You Tarzan. Me Jane.

MARILYN. (lunging for her) How would you like a quick punch in the kidneys.

LUCY. (distressed) Oh you <u>guys</u>. Stop. She'll get us all if we're fighting when she comes in.

BETTY. Come on. We better play something else.

ALICE. (efficiently) What about Looby Loo?

BETTY. Good idea. Into a circle everybody.

(They form a circle and skip round singing)

ALL.
    Here we go Looby Loo
    Here we go Looby Light
    Here we go Looby Loo
    All on a Saturday night.
    You put your right leg in
    You take your right leg out
    You give your leg a shake shake shake
    And turn yourselves about.

(Sound of footsteps outside. They circle round again accelerating)

ALICE. (loud whisper) Smile! Smile!

ALL. (fast and with hectic gaiety)
    Here we go Looby Loo Here we go Looby
    Light Here we go Looby -

(The door opens and the MATRON in a white coat and dark glasses comes in and fires a pistol three times into the air. The girls all scream and gasp and fall on the floor. Then crawl together into a huddled group staring at the MATRON)

MATRON. (speaking as always in a very mannered and somehow weird way) And if you think that I think that that is how you spend your time in here you are wrong. Table. (Nods to DOTTY)

   (DOTTY scrambles over, gets it, sets it carefully and precisely in front of the chair and then dashes back to the others. The MATRON sits and gets a notebook out of her pocket)

MATRON. Roll call. Addison.

LUCY. (quavers) Here.

MATRON. Hayes.

ALICE. Here.

MATRON. Channing.

MARILYN. Here.

MATRON. Jordan.

BETTY. Here.

MATRON. Starr.

DOTTY. Here.

MATRON. Menlo.

KAY. Here.

   (The MATRON closes the book, sighs, looks over at them)

MATRON. (irritably) Why are you all huddled up over there? Come and sit where you belong. You're making me nervous.

   (They all move over warily and sit crosslegged in a semi circle on the floor in front of her)

135

MARILYN. (as they move. Mutters it) We're making you nervous.

MATRON. (sharp) Did you speak, Channing?

MARILYN. (stammering) No Matron. I didn't.

MATRON. (grim smile) I'm so glad. (Puts her palms hard against her temples) Oh my head...my head. (Pauses. Looks at the girls) I have had a piece of extremely disturbing information today, the import of which is so crucial that I cannot yet speak of it. I must be calmed. Soothed. Sing me something. Something from the Bard.

(The girls shift uneasily. Clear their throats)

(Exasperated) Shakespeare! (Takes off her glasses and leans her elbow on the table, shielding her eyes with her hand. Snaps her fingers) Quickly!

LUCY. (speaks rather hysterically, getting up onto her knees) Well I'm not going to sing. Shooting at us! It's against the law. I'm going to write to my Senator. It's unethical - it's -

MATRON. (not looking up) Addison.

LUCY. (nervously defiant) Yes?

MATRON. I suppose you think this pistol is loaded with blanks.

MARILYN. Of course she does. It is. You wouldn't dare, you wouldn't!

(She is interrupted. The MATRON swiftly puts on her glasses, takes out the pistol and shoots at the candle in the corner. Candle and holder are blown off the box. The girls gasp. The MATRON puts the pistol on the table in front of her, takes off her glasses and resumes her pose)

MATRON. (wearily peremptory) Sing.

(LUCY starts falteringly and the rest follow. They sing 'Full Fathom Five', the Dr. Arne setting. When they reach the last 'Ding Dong Bell' they stop)

(Not moving. Through her teeth) More. I prithee more.

DOTTY.
Ding dong dell
Pussy's in the well.

BETTY.
Who threw her in?
Little Tommy Thin.

ALICE.
Who got her out?
Little Tommy Stout.

MARILYN.
Wasn't that a naughty boy
To drown poor pussy cat

KAY.
Who ne'er did any harm

LUCY.
But killed all the mice in Father's barn.

(Again they fall silent. The MATRON doesn't move)

KAY. (leading off with a kind of mad heartiness)
Into the air Junior Birdmen.

OTHERS.
Into the air, Birdmen true.
Into the air, Junior Birdmen
And keep your eyes up in the blue -

MATRON. (puts on glasses again) Be quiet.

(They trail nervously off)

Now. This news. Pay attention please. I do not intend

to repeat anything. The information came to me at
1300 hours today by cablegram from Uruguay. I
have checked it out. It is authentic. One of you girls
is my own child and therefore sane.

(There is absolute silence. The MATRON does not
seem disposed to continue. After a pause DOTTY
speaks ingratiatingly)

DOTTY. I didn't even know you were married, Matron.

MATRON. I am not. The incident occurred when I was a
novice in a Carmelite convent near Fresno.

(Again she stops)

KAY. Uh...incident, Matron?

MATRON. (sighs with a kind of impatience. Then speaks)
It was approximately ten o'clock in the morning. I was
out tilling the fields. Or some such. The morning was
misty but it was going to be a very hot day. My habit
hung heavy on me and I could feel the sweat beginning
to trickle already between my breasts down to my
navel. (She stops again)

ALICE. Yes?

MATRON. I found myself humming as I hoed - a little
hymn I had learned as a girl scout. Something about a
garden. I cannot at the moment recall the opening
phrases but I had just come to the bit that went (Talks
it) And he walked with me and he talked with me and
he told me I was his own. And the joy we shared in
the garden there, no other has ever -' And then
suddenly he appeared.

(Again she stops dead)

BETTY. Who Matron? Who appeared?

MATRON. (touch impatient) Jesus, as I thought at the
time, Jordan. Our Lord. Although I was mistaken
as matters subsequently fell out. (Stops again)

KAY. And then what happened, Matron?

MATRON. (pinching the bridge of her nose with finger and thumb, eyes closed) It is painful for me to continue.

MARILYN. (soft) Please Matron.

OTHERS. Please.

MATRON. (clasping her hands together. Gazing upwards) It is not easy to be a nun. I had been instructed, yes, but not in the sphere which I was now so precipitously to confront. My own mother had told me nothing - nothing! My father, too, had remained silent. True, he had passed away when I was three weeks old but still (Then fiercely) Be fruitful and multiply by all means but not secretive. The facts should be passed on - (Thoughtful) - or the bare outlines at any rate. I was as innocent as a snowdrop. I was a spring crocus without a compass.

DOTTY. Poor Matron.

OTHERS. Poor Matron.

DOTTY. (fairly avid) And then?

MATRON. And then, Starr, then - after we had passed a word or two about the coming elections, the recent forest fires, he (Pauses) hurled me down between the rows of sugar beets and...and...

LUCY. (wide eyed) And Had His Way With You?

MATRON. (exhausted) In a nutshell, Addison. You have hit the nail on the head.

ALICE. And one of us.....?

MATRON. And one of you, Hayes, yes one of you very girls is the precipitant as you might say of that catastrophic and uncalled for chemical combination.

(She gets up, moved, and walks about)

I sped to my confessor eager to speak of this - this
Visitation. He, after a brisk conference with the
Mother Superior, had me dispatched to a nursing home
in Twin Falls, Idaho. Some months later I was, to my
astonishment, delivered of a female child. The infant
was adopted, I left the order and applied successfully
for my present post in this institution. (Pause) There
My story is told.

(She falls silent again, her back to the girls. They look
at each other. Then KAY gets to her feet. Speaks
formally)

KAY. Matron, I would just like to say that I know I speak
for us all in expressing our sympathy.

OTHERS. (warmly) Hear hear.

MATRON. (turning round) Shut up. And you Menlo, sit
down. I'm in charge here. I'm not remotely interested
in your sympathy. The question is now simply one of
procedure. One of you - my progeny - is sane. It is
not, of course, possible that I could have produced a
mentally unstable child.

MARILYN. Maybe he could've, though.

MATRON. (smoothly dangerous) Just watch it, Channing.
(Fingers pistol in her pocket. Then businesslike) You
will all take turns to attempt to prove your sanity in
order that the necessary consanguinity can be finally
established.

LUCY. (leaping up) It's me, Matron. I'm your daughter.
I've always felt close to you - always. My parents told
me when I was four that I'd been adopted and I've got
this locket with a piece of hair in it - yours Matron,
I know it, I know it! And I've got a strawberry mark
on my left buttock - shall I show you?

MATRON. That will do, Addison, thank you. I have no wish
to see either of your buttocks; my child was without
blemish and I have never in my life had any truck with
lockets. Now. Jordan.

BETTY. (rising) I know that I am sane, Matron. My
mother was not my real mother although she never
admitted it. She hated me. She wanted me to become a
Business Consultant and because my own ambition was
to be a veterinary surgeon, she had me certified. Would
a real mother have done such a thing? Isn't a Vet more
important than a Business Consultant?

MATRON. The answer to your first question is yes and to
the second certainly not. Man is the noblest creature in
the universe and the intricacies of his daily work far
more important than the physiological difficulties of
the beasts his servants. Read your Leviticus. And sit
down. Hayes?

ALICE. (clears throat) Angostura aromatic bitters was
first made in 1924 by Dr. J.G.B. Siegert in the town
of Angostura Venezuela. It is now produced by
Angostura Bitters (Dr. J.G.B. Siegert & Sons Ltd, the
successors of Dr. J.G.B. Siegert) in Port of Spain,
Trinidad, West Indies, from his original recipe.
Aromatic Angostura Bitters may be distinguished from
all other aromatic bitters by its fine flavour and
aromatic odour. At the principal International Exhibi-
tions it has received the highest recognitions. Because
of its delightful flavour and aroma it has become
extremely popular for use in soft drinks, cocktails and
other alcoholic beverages. It also imparts an exquisite
flavour to soups, salads, vegetables, gravies, fish,
grapefruit, mixed cut fruits, stewed prunes, stewed
figs, preserved fruits, jellies, sherbets, water ices,
ice creams, sauces for puddings, hard sauces, plum
puddings, mince and fruit pies, apple sauce and all
similar desserts. Regulating the quantity according to
taste. And I can say it in three different languages.
Could a mad person do that?

MATRON. Would a sane one want to. Down. Starr?

DOTTY. (standing up and gabbling) I always say please and
thank you. I've never wet my pants in my whole life
and I wash my hands every time I go to the bathroom.
I never take the last cookie on the plate. I believe
everything my elders and betters tell me and I always

always do what I'm told. That's sane isn't it?

MATRON. No, Starr, that is capital M madness. What we call the real McCoy. Channing?

MARILYN. (stands up and speaks very simply) I'm the only one who could be your real daughter, Matron, you know that.

MATRON. Why should I know that?

MARILYN. Simple. I'm as mean as you are. That's how I know that other woman wasn't my mother at all. She was soft and she was a liar. She used to tell me I was pretty. She said to me once - she was crazy all right - 'You've got cold hands but that means you've got a warm heart.' Really nutty, see. I'm not pretty and I never will be and (Rubbing her hands together) I do have cold hands but I don't have a warm heart. (Stops. Takes a deep breath. Then speaks flatly) I'm mean and nobody likes me - just like you are.

MATRON. (almost gently) Just sit down, Channing. Just sit down. .....Menlo?

KAY. Well it has to be me anyway, doesn't it - if it isn't any of them. I could prove I was sane but how could they understand it because they're crazy. I could say a couple of things like - well - like, most people think there's an up and a down and an inside and an outside and a good and an evil but they're wrong. 'Jesus said to them: When you make the two one, and when you make the inner as the outer and the outer as the inner and the above as the below, and when you make the male and the female into a single one so that the male will not be male and the female not be female, when you make eyes in the place of an eye, and a hand in the place of a hand and a foot in the place of a foot, and an image in the place of an image then shall you enter the kingdom'. Read your gospel according to Thomas.

MATRON. Don't be sassy with me, Menlo. Only mad people quote the Bible. I referred; I did not quote. Besides, the Thomas Gospel is extra-canonical.

(KAY goes up to her and speaks slowly and strongly right into her face)

KAY. You're saying that we are all mad then.

MATRON. (After a pause. In girl's voice) Well wait a second. I haven't had my turn yet. (Takes off white coat and glasses. She is dressed as the others) Who's going to be me?

MARILYN. (jumps up and snatches the coat) I will, Elly. (Speaks in bad imitation of ELLY's Matron voice) Now then, Claremont, state your case.

ELLY. (crossly. Taking the coat) Give it back. You're no good at it, Marilyn, and you know it.

KAY. I will.

BETTY. No, I want to.

DOTTY. No, me.

ALICE. Me.

ELLY. (overriding. Loud) Will you all just shut up, all of you! I'll choose. I'm the authority!

(There is immediately a very uneasy silence. All the girls look about. Not at each other)

(Uncertain) I mean...I mean...the authority on the Matron. I made her up, after all. I - I - I am the authority.

(And at once the bell rings in the distance but louder this time. They all jump)

MARILYN. (angry whisper to ELLY) Big mouth!

LUCY. The bell would have gone anyway, Elly, it's just the bedtime bell. It always goes at the same time.

DOTTY. We have to stop.

ALICE. You've missed your turn, Elly. <u>And</u> you take too many chances.

LUCY. I'm sure nobody heard her.

MARILYN. Like who would that be?

BETTY. Lay off her, Marilyn. (The bell goes again, even louder) Come on you all. That's the last bell.

(They all start to move towards the door. ELLY packs away the Matron gear)

LUCY. I do like it here - really I do.

ALICE. We all do, dopey.

DOTTY. Yeah, that's right, but the thing is though (Pause) I can't remember when I came here. Can you, Lucy?

KAY. Shut up you two, will you. Just shut up. We don't need to know any of that.

LUCY. (to BETTY. By now they are all out of the room but LUCY and BETTY) Does anybody know?

BETTY. Know what?

LUCY. Know <u>why</u>.

BETTY. (touching her in some nice, gentle but matter of fact way) No. Nobody does.

(And they go out the door and shut it and the lights fade)

CURTAIN